Praise for LIBRE

"We are enveloped in a blanket of fears, insecurities, anxieties, and feelings that blind us from seeing our own inner beauty, from where our happiness really lies. Free is a book that can be used as a tool to bring us closer to the answers we are seeking, to find freedom from the many blocks we have created over the years. This book will certainly bring light for many, it is full of practical exercises to improve our lives".

Catalina Vargas, *Health Coach* - www.cataploom.com

"If you are thinking whether to read this book or not, my advice is: do it. There is no better counselor than one who has lived the process in her own flesh. It is the case with this book, in which Paola presents her experience. Between practical advice and anecdotes with clear purposes, she guides us to continuously improve, be free, and choose our destiny. When you read this book, you will recognize Paola's style immediately. Teaching us to constantly discover new ways to grow and enjoy life to the fullest. It is precisely this style that makes her an example to follow for all those who have the pleasure of knowing her. So I recommend that you read, enjoy, grow, embrace life, and be free".

Amado Sánchez, *Executive Coach* - www.dilectus.net

"The Author Paola Castro shares her essence in this book and more than that, this book is an offering for life. It invites us to "stop" in order to discover the power of self-realization, fulfillment, freedom, and LOVE. I know you will enjoy it."

Stephanie Fallas Navarro, *Business and Life Coach & Organizational Consultant*

"FREE - just by reading the first few pages of this book that is filled with love created a shift inside of me. As Paola says: one tends to think that once everything is fixed and perfect we are going to be happy, when in reality by believing this we are in fact distancing ourselves from self-love. Reading this book is a liberation. Thanks to Paola for sharing her journey and for being an example for all of us."

Fabiola Rumich, *Personal Branding Coach* - www.fabiolarumich.com

FREE

YOUR PATH TO FULFILLMENT BEGINS HERE

PAOLA CASTRO

San José, Costa Rica.

Costa Rican Essay / Personal Development

Translator: Ana Fonseca

Collaborators: Nicholas Barnett, Nicole Rager and Steve Walton

Photography: Luke Vanis

Design, layout and printing: eStudio G

estudiog13@gmail.com

To my family, without you my life would not be a song filled with love, peace, kindness and grace.
To my tribe , thank you for walking with me in this very human and beautiful journey.
And to Spirit, eternally grateful for unconditionally loving me.

TABLE OF CONTENTS

You don't have a soul.
You are a soul.
You have a body.
C. S. Lewis

PROLOGUE

Many of us have experienced great cultural conditioning based on fear, shame, and guilt. The opposite of those three states is what I call " freedom."

You may wonder: How can I know that fear, shame, and guilt affect me? My answer is simple: If you feel inadequate.

Why do we have this feeling of inadequacy? Because we have not learned - nor have we taken the time to do so - to be our own personal historians. We don't know our own individual stories because we are still trapped within them by giving meaning to what we believe is our destiny or our reality.

The story and exercises that Paola Castro will share with you will remind you of your formative years and experiences, challenging your perceptions and sharing exercises that you can follow to change your beliefs, attitudes, and emotions.

There is a big difference between knowing something and doing something: one is conceptual and the other is a process of self-exploration. Until you have done your part and lived the experience, you won't see evidence of your evolution.

And, where do we begin with the process of self-discovery? Most of the time, we start with the discomfort, the pain, and regret.

That said, there are two roles in life: the passive and the proactive role. You can choose to be the victim to whom "life happens," or you can choose to be the hero who transforms destiny to his whim and makes lemonade with the lemons of life. These are two different journeys. Either way, your life is what it is, and it is up to you to find the most beneficial beliefs and meanings that will help you create a more rewarding future.

If you want to be proactive about your personal development and your healing process, read FREE and enjoy the journey of transformation that this book gives you.

MICHAEL J. EMERY

INTRODUCTION

For so long I was trapped between the mind and the body! Just thinking, thrilled, that if I had everything planned, organized, and understood, that life would certainly be easier. Sure, that happened to me, but to a lesser extent than desired, the more I tried, the farther away I found myself from my self-worth.

I read books, I went to seminars, I did everything, and even then, I never understood why it was so difficult to be free.

Until one day I realized that fear is only an illusion that covers our physical eyes with a veil and does not let us see the truth.

My truth, your truth, the Universe's truth.

With this book, not only do I want to tell you about my ongoing journey toward wholeness and freedom, but I also want you to seize my words in your heart so that you, too, can embark on your journey, with an intent and an open heart to listen, to understand, and to practice what I am about to share with you.

Let´s begin.

Love is what we are born with. Fear is what we learn.
The spiritual journey is the unlearning of fear and
prejudices and the acceptance of love back in our hearts.
Love is the essential reality and our purpose on earth.
To be consciously aware of it, to experience love in
ourselves and others, is the meaning of life.
Meaning does not lie in things.
Meaning lies in us.

MARIANNE WILLIAMSON

Chapter I

THE VEIL

We are born in this world destined to be programmed: by our surroundings, our genetics and our culture.

At school we are told: “We are born, we grow, we reproduce, and we die.” Perceived from a physical standpoint, it is true. Thanks to my story, my parents’ story and that of others who have challenged their programming, today, I know that this simplistic way of grasping our destiny can be changed, which allows us to move from a way of being to a way of transcending.

What happens is that we cannot even think about transcending if we do not understand the veil that covers our spiritual eyes from the truth of our existence.

Let´s begin with contrast. We have night and day, yin and yang, man and woman, good and evil. This is the natural contrast that upholds balance. To know light, we must know darkness, to enjoy happiness, we must undergo moments of sadness. To program ourselves, we must first be initially deprogrammed.

Such programming can then be understood in two ways. First, had we not been programmed, we could not have lived on this planet, since we would not be able to socialize, to make choices, or even to speak our country’s language; second, because of this programming, we have unlearned who we really are. When we are born, everything is clear, in terms of peace, fulfillment and happiness. Just take a look at a baby and you will be able to see how his/her magnetism causes adults to be in a state of admiration.

By being children - at least until two years of age - we perceive the world without prejudice, we simply are, we are in complete harmony with the Source that created us. We accept the uncertainty, since our lack of conscience forces us to trust those who take care of us.

With time, amnesia eclipses the infant's overflowing joy. When we begin to process information, we see that this world is perhaps not as safe as we thought, maybe our guardians are not as shielding as we hoped. As we begin to encounter situations of uncertainty, we create a self-protective cloud of knowledge in our brain that causes us to forget the infinite capacity of our existence.

Once we process this information, we know what keeps us safe and what does not. At that moment, we are already conditioned by our own mind to react in certain ways under certain circumstances, after all, its task is to keep us alive. So, it is then that we start to choose our life based on knowledge that is acquired or transferred to us.

We find ourselves in a society where adults perceive that they must change, improve or find something that they lost. We know that this feeling of *emptiness* is not what we deserve.

The good news is that nothing has been lost, we do not need to change or become something that we are not, but, rather, we must remember who we are and release our perfect essence, the same one that has been hiding under layers of protection and fear.

With this book, I intend to guide you to lift the veil of logic and resistance. To help you remember who you really are. Just like I have remembered. Today I feel the calling to pass that memory down to you, to transmit it and for you to pass it on to others until we create a beautiful revolution, the same one that is already spreading around the world. **The awakening of consciousness.**

Something that I wish to warn you of, before we continue, is that this book was not created as a magic potion that you take only once and everything is resolved. This is a daily practice, a new lifestyle. The intent of this book is for you to remember who you are, again and again, so that you can live a full life in complete alignment with your essence. This is a bedside book.

Nothing is lost. Everything is still inside. Together, we are going to unravel the layers of illusion, for you to claim your birthright: To live a life that makes your heart sing!

WE BEGIN BY CONFESSING

Then you will know the truth, and the truth will set you free.
John 8:32

Just like a high-rise building, we need a deep, strong foundation to hold up what we are about to build.

Let´s start with this: "The truth sets me free." I repeat these words over and over, every time I feel I am not aligned with myself.

What does it mean to not be aligned? It is when you feel frustrated, hopeless, negative and unwilling to do what you know you must do to take steps toward your evolution.

That is why it is important to confess. For me, to confess means to be honest with oneself and express what is bothering you or what you are longing for, with all your heart, but for some reason is not present in your life, either because you have run from it due to fear of not being deserving or of not being able to achieve it.

So, in order to begin to feel less weight on yourself, you must learn to confess, not with a priest or with a psychologist, but with yourself, in solitude, in front of a mirror, or with your pillow, privately.

Let´s start small, to be kind to ourselves.

With great caution we hide our insecurities, and for that reason we are now going to uncover them with caution as well. What do we not dare say out loud? Below are some of my examples, as well as others I have heard from my clients:

"I am not good enough to take this job"

"I do not think I am good enough to be liked by the man or the woman of my dreams"

"I am not as smart as other people so I won't be able to get as far as I want to go"

"I am not sure I want to continue to be in a relationship"

"I do not want to stay at this job anymore, but I am afraid that I won't get another one"

"I do not want to continue with this project, it doesn't inspire me and I don't feel passionate about it"

"I want to study something different from what I chose, but I am ashamed of what people may say/think"

"I know I have to take care of my body, but I prefer to ignore my reality, it is too hard to face what I have done to myself"

"My marriage is not going well"

"I feel guilty for not being what I think I should be, for example: be a better mom/dad, daughter/son, girlfriend/ boyfriend, employee, etc."

...among many more "confessions" we do not want to face.

We must challenge ourselves to confront what we are running from because therein lies the secret to establishing a solid foundation, a base with roots of authenticity.

We must dare to see ourselves as we are. It is a small but powerful step; it opens doors and possibilities. Little by little, you will find the courage to take conscientious actions, to leave behind what you previously believed you could never release.

In my coaching sessions, I invite my clients to gradually confess to themselves their most embarrassing thoughts. These are the kinds of thoughts that you want to deny or run away, and hide from whenever you think of them.

If we do not do this, then we will continue to lie to ourselves, until one day we are unable to differentiate between the truth of our soul and an imposed truth, born of the need to stay in the comfort zone, seeking to please others, or simply out of fear of what people might say.

For this reason, I invite you to whisper your truth. Do not tell anyone yet, but I am sure that by reading this, you will know where your truth lies.

The courage to take our fears and to look them straight in the eyes instead of fleeing from them creates a miracle, one that I call "the death of the illusion of fear and the resurrection of the truth: love".

Free Writing Exercise:

Do this, preferably in a place where you will not be interrupted. I recommend you do this every day until you connect deeply with yourself.

Place your left hand on your heart and your right hand on your stomach, right on your belly-button. Breathe deeply through your nose and exhale through your mouth. Do this for 1 minute on the first day and increase the time each day you practice it. Pay attention to your breathing and your heartbeat. Once you are connected with your heartbeat and your breathing, repeat this phrase in your mind, "I am willing to listen to the truth of my soul."

Wait serenely and let your heart tell you what is really happening. This may take a few minutes or even days. We have been practicing for so long the art of not listening to ourselves. Be patient.

Once you do this, you are going to take a pen and on the page below you will write at the top.

Dear (your name):
I am your soul and I want to tell you the following:

In this space, please give yourself a few minutes. Set a timer for 1 to 5 minutes, as long as you can, and write freely, with your mind only loosely focused on the writing itself. For example, it does not matter if in the beginning you write: *"I want to tell you that.... I do not know how to do this exercise, but I'm going to give myself the chance to write, write what's inside of me..."* and you continue without paying attention to your grammar, or if what you are writing makes sense or not. Let it flow like we did when we were children, improvising. Let yourself go, write freely.

This free form of writing gives you access to your soul's wisdom, which is why it is important that you do this without thinking and without stopping. In this manner, the mind will not manipulate the message.

CHAPTER II

WAKE UP

Where are you today?

Some time ago during a seminar, the lecturer did an exercise that changed my belief on the role that my heart plays in life. Since then, I frequently ask participants in my own workshops to do the same exercise.

This practice is very simple. It consists of asking people to point to themselves with their hand and state, "This is me!" The amazing thing is that when they do this, they immediately point toward their heart.

We all have the so-called "inner voice," that part of us that *knows*, that understands very clearly when something is not aligned with what we want in life. The voice is always there, even if we sometimes decide to silence it or have become experts in doing so.

I say this with conviction because I, myself, have been an expert in doing so. Since I was a little girl, I learned the importance of liking others before I liked myself. I learned that if I did what was expected of me, I would be rewarded with acceptance; contrarily, if I expressed less positive emotions, I would be rejected.

My parents were wonderful and loving parents and they did the best they could. They certainly did much better than their parents did with them. Even so, the system is built to raise children conditioned with certain behaviors in order to produce socially adapted people, and this gradually confines their authenticity.

As adults, we say *Yes* when we really mean *No*, and we say *No* when we really mean *Yes*. We accept a certain job because we believe there is no better option, although we know it is not what we actually want. The same holds true of romantic relationships, friendships, unnecessary expenditures we make. The list is endless.

But there is always an inner voice within us. I call it *intuition, will, infinite wisdom* or *inner guidance* that, as mentioned above, is very pure when we are children, but as we grow older, we begin to silence it, until one day it becomes difficult to differentiate intuition from fear. Although we deal with these two elements of ourselves every day, sometimes situations are greater than a passing circumstance.

A few years ago I found myself in such a situation. After some time of using what they call "logic" to choose what was right, instead of what I really felt and wanted, I built for myself the picture-perfect scenario: I met the perfect man, who gave me the perfect love, the perfect house, the perfect lifestyle, and my inevitable calling should have been to live happily ever after. He was a great person, and my situation was enviable, but I sensed deep down that something was not in alignment.

We did not share the same key values that were important, we did not have a "soulmate" connection.

However,I continued to ignore my deepest and truest emotions, which were revealing that this was not in fact the journey I so wanted.

It took me a while to listen to my inner voice, but it became apparent during my coaching certification process, when I went through a complete catharsis in my life, the denial could continue no more. Little by little, I began to confess to myself what I was terrified to accept. And you know what? It was not easy. Each day that I confronted my situation was one day closer to making the decision to end my relationship, one that I had believed would last forever.

It took me ten long months, but I finally did it. In the end, I began to understand what true freedom was, that kind of freedom that lets you go to sleep every night with a peaceful and quiet conscience.

Similarly, I have been in jobs completely removed from my essence, in toxic friendships and unhealthy habits that hurt my body and my mind.

All of the above have been lessons learned and actions taken that took place over a period of time, so I do not encourage you to immediately give up your jobs, break up with your partners or drop your friends. The secret is not to give up; the secret is to start off with the truth and see where our inner voice takes us.

I promise you, this shall lead us to peace and fulfillment.

Now it´s your turn:

I want to share one of the simplest, yet most powerful exercises.

This exercise gave me the opportunity to see my life as a *whole*, as a perfect orchestra that needs all of its instruments playing harmoniously and pleasantly together.

That is what we want; for your life to be in harmony with all that you desire.

Wheel of Life:

Think about each aspect of your life. Here, assess on a scale from 1 to 10, how you feel in each area (1 being "I feel very bad/unstable" and 10 "I feel great").

Now, notice and ask yourself:

What were the two areas with the lowest score?

What are the two areas that you would like to change or improve? (They do not necessarily have to be the ones with the lowest scores).

Tip: If you are not sure which areas of your life to choose, ask yourself: What do you constantly think about? What thoughts come to mind when you wake up in the morning and go to sleep at night? To which aspect of your life do these thoughts or worries belong to?

How would you be feeling if these two areas were a 10?

What small actions can you take in these areas to take steps toward your freedom?

It is important that we see our life as a whole. By improving one area, everything else is transformed as well, a beautiful example of symbiosis. A small ray of light is able to brighten an entire space.

WHAT ARE YOU NOT ACCEPTING?

Life is simple. Everything happens for you, not to you. Everything happens at exactly the right moment, neither too soon nor too late. You don't have to like it... it's just easier if you do.

BYRON KATIE

We always know when we do not want to accept something. If there was a college degree called *Master in Dodging Reality with emphasis on non-acceptance*, surely a few years ago I would have graduated with honors; starting with friends who robbed my energy, to meaningless jobs and purposeless relationships. That is why I have had to learn to tell the truth.

In my case, I was raised in a quiet family unit. My parents always strived for my brother and I to never see them fighting. This undoubtedly boosted my emotional balance. Still, by not witnessing expressions of anger or frustration, I grew up thinking that this must be the natural state of everything. In life, not everything is black or white. There is a whole range of colors in the middle. I am happy not to have seen my parents fight, but indisputably, to know that feelings like anger or frustration are very human emotions, when they are channeled right, would have been healthier.

Now, three decades later, I can say that I have learned to live in the midst of these colors, without feeding my fears or immersing myself in evasive positivism. When you argue with "what is," says author, Byron Katie, in her remarkable book, *Loving What Is*, you lose only 100% of the time; nonetheless, we are experts in not accepting, in struggling with "what is" and living anguished and victimized by circumstances.

Humans were given an inner guide system, which we have access to 24 hours a day, 7 days a week. This system is such wonderful and perfect technology that it would take us a long time to create a similar one. This inner guide is called: "Our Rainbow of Emotions." Yes! Our emotions are a direct access to our intuition, to our truth. So, I want you to return to the previous page, to the wheel of life, and write down next to each area of your life: how do I feel TODAY in each one of them?

Go for it! Do not read on if you have not done the exercise. I will be waiting for you here.

Ready?

Take a good look at each of the areas in your life. How do you feel concerning each one and what are your feelings telling you?

If you feel stuck at your job, then that may be your inner guidance telling you the following:

—I am not happy with this job.

—I would like to pursue another career.

—I want to start looking at other companies.
—It is time to talk to my boss.
—It is time to be more assertive.
—It is time to look at that business idea again.
—It is time to ask for a promotion.

Let's apply this thought process to the other areas of your life.

Perhaps, regarding your relationship/love, you might say: I do not feel fulfilled.

Then, ask that emotion, "What are you telling me?" And most likely the response will be something like this:

—This relationship needs a greater purpose.
—My fears are growing, I need to feel safe.
—We don't have the same values.
—I want to be single.
—It is time to seek professional help because we are not doing well.
—Our communication needs attention, etc.

Now, let's move from an external outlook to a more internal perspective.

What things about yourself are you not accepting?

For example, I grew up with the notion that I was emotionally balanced; that the way I saw things was the way they were. The impression that I had no areas to improve, besides being arrogant, caused me to make mistakes and then realize that there were actually emotional traces that I needed to heal.

The most important thing about this exercise is to allow the emotion to guide us to where the truth lies and what is it that we are not accepting.

When I asked myself these questions, at first, I did not want to accept the answers. My resistance was too strong to realize that the life I had built for myself from the time I was a child was nothing more than a social victory, not an inner success story. My soul never lied to me, nor did it stop talking to me; I was the one who learned to silence it, to fill myself with outside noise so I would not have to pay attention to the truth, and now, I had to give its deserving voice back in order to achieve what I wanted. It was a very difficult step, but I promise you: this is a step toward freedom.

Take your time, do not hurry! This is the first step, and perhaps the most important. Accepting *what is* is not something that you achieve overnight. While it is true that sometimes we have those "magical" moments, in which everything suddenly falls into place and the truth set us free, we do not necessarily have to expect and wait for that to happen in order to find our way toward authenticity.

OUR EMOTIONAL WOUNDS

In his book, *The Mastery of Love,* Miguel Ruiz says that we, human beings, are born with an unharmed emotional body, but as time goes by, the first wounds begin to appear on our bodies, to the point that if someone wants to touch us, we immediately react with pain. It might seem difficult to accept certain things about our reality, because to accept them is like pouring salt in the wound. We have emotional wounds that we do not even know we have and these keep us from discovering the truth.

I am not a psychoanalyst and in my coaching sessions I focus mainly on the following: Where we are today and where we want to go tomorrow. Moreover, I acknowledge the importance of searching where these wounds came from and how they can be healed.

When I was younger, I thought I was a normal person living in a normal world. My outlook changed year after year, as if I were experiencing a butterfly's metamorphosis. The crises, the pains and the trials of the world began to awaken me. So, I decided to use these ordeals to come to life and not drift off any longer.

That is why I take this opportunity to tell my story:

I grew up in a middle-class family, with loving parents, strong spiritual beliefs and practices. I was born seven years later than my brother, at a time when my mom was graduating from college. It was a very difficult time for her, since my arrival was not planned and that changed the course of her life. Naturally, my brother felt jealous with my presence, and true to form, as I grew older, I was constantly rejected by him. My mom worked a lot and my dad, as a business owner, had more time for my brother and me, but he, too, had to work. Several housemaids contributed to my education and upbringing. I grew up watching *telenovelas* (soap operas) and elements such as structure and discipline were not very present in my life.

Then again, my parents did what they could and spoiling me and my brother is what they did best.

I was born with a small defect in my kidneys and before I was even a month old, I had to spend extra time in the hospital. When I was able to go home, my mother, full of guilt, decided to pamper me, and one of her demonstrations of love was to overfeed me so I would recover all the weight I had lost during my hospitalization. As a result, I became an overweight girl. Which, even without my understanding, seemed to be a big problem for the world.

My aunts, uncles, cousins and other relatives, along with my classmates had a big problem with me being different. I did not understand it very well, but upon entering puberty, I decided that if it was a problem for others, it was going to be a problem for me, too. Thus began years of rejecting my body. As I grew older, it was my understanding that beauty meant being worthy of love. If I was not beautiful, I was not good enough.

Because of these beliefs, I accepted unhealthy relationships, and I carried these insecurities in all areas of my life. As expected in a young woman keen to discover the world, I drank and partied starting at a very young age, and although I do not have an addictive personality, I did have episodes of not being in control. This continued until my early twenties, when I began to discover that there were other ways of living and finding love in the right places.

It was then that my healing process began.

My purpose and hope in writing this book is that you do not take so long to begin using this knowledge and tools to also heal yourself from within.

IS IT POSSIBLE TO CHANGE?

Logic will get you from A to B.
Imagination will take you everywhere.
ALBERT EINSTEIN

A great friend once told me: "We human beings are intellectually dishonest, because by using our intellectual logic we betray the truth of our heart." That is so true! We follow the rules literally and logically and then we find ourselves feeling that somehow we have landed in the wrong place.

We do not know why we feel such emptiness if what we have done so far is exactly what we were "supposed" to do. Once we begin the path of authenticity, we can then begin to ask ourselves: what would happen if ________________ is something I want? Just allow yourself to daydream, do not take action if you do not feel ready. For now, we are only lifting the veil before us.

WHAT IS IT THAT YOU WANT?

You don´t know? In that case, I have an exercise that you will give you greater clarity.

First, make a list of what you DO NOT want. Then, write the opposite. For survival reasons, our brain is designed to detect what is not right, what we do not have, and what we are not. This allows us to remain alert to any threat or danger. So let's use that to our advantage.

For example, a few years ago, this was my list:

1. I do not want to work on something that I am not passionate about, that has no relevance with who I am and that pays me poorly.
2. I do not want to be in a relationship in which my love is not reciprocated, or vice versa.
3. I do not want financial troubles or to experience moments of scarcity.
4. I do not want to continue rejecting my body anymore, and feel like I overeat in a cycle of self-sabotage.
5. I do not want to continue to seek well-being outside of my life (in alcohol, cigarettes, relationships, approval of others, etc.).
6. I do not want to live in the city.
7. I do not want to give up my dream of writing a book.
8. I do not want to have toxic relationships.
9. I do not want to be overwhelmed by fear.

10. I do not want to feel bad for long periods of time.

Then, for each statement, I wrote the opposite:

1. I want to create a job in which I feel passionate, purposeful and prosperous.
2. I want to have a loving, reciprocal, synergistic, and spiritual relationship.
3. I want financial freedom and abundant resources.
4. I want to love my body, listen to it, and eat the necessary nutrients to make it vibrant.
5. I want to find well-being and love in my connection with Source before resorting to external means in order to fill any emptiness.
6. I want to live at the beach.
7. I want to finish and publish my book.
8. I want to have cordial, loving, and true interpersonal relationships.
9. I want love and compassion to steer my life.
10. I want feeling good to be my #1 priority so that when I feel disconnected from the truth, I am more able to consciously return to it.

The previous exercise is extremely powerful because it allows you to understand several things:

1. Life teaches us, through adversity, exactly what we DO NOT want.

2. By knowing what we DO NOT want, we can be clearer about what we DO want.

3. When we begin to inquire into what we DO want, our imagination becomes restless, our soul is heartened and we begin to vibrate with a stronger and more magnetic energy.

4. By focusing on what we want, we are activating the law of manifestation and everything that vibrates with that energy will be attracted to us.

Now, it is your turn to do it and begin to discover what it is that you really want!

WHAT I DO NOT WANT:

1. ____________________
2. ____________________
3. ____________________
4. ____________________
5. ____________________
6. ____________________
7. ____________________
8. ____________________
9. ____________________
10. ____________________
11. ____________________
12. ____________________
13. ____________________
14. ____________________
15. ____________________
16. ____________________
17. ____________________
18. ____________________
19. ____________________
20. ____________________

THE OPPOSITE OF MY STATEMENTS:

1. ______________________________
2. ______________________________
3. ______________________________
4. ______________________________
5. ______________________________
6. ______________________________
7. ______________________________
8. ______________________________
9. ______________________________
10. ______________________________
11. ______________________________
12. ______________________________
13. ______________________________
14. ______________________________
15. ______________________________
16. ______________________________
17. ______________________________
18. ______________________________
19. ______________________________
20. ______________________________

FEAR (THE ILLUSION)

Perfect love casts out fear.
If fear exists, then there is no perfect love.
A Course in Miracles

In life, there are fears that we intrinsically have and others that we pick up over time. There are many lines of thought on the subject of fear; personally, I define it as **an emotion that can guide us in life if we allow it to be merely the co-pilot of our life and not the driver.** Biologically, fear can be defined as our sense of survival. Some time ago, I learned about an effect termed by scientists as "the fight-or-flight response". This response carries an extensive explanation but I will tell you my short and simple version.

Hundreds of years ago, our ancestors lived in rather hostile environments, in which they were required to hunt and tackle challenging climates to survive. In our brain, we have a gland called the amygdala, which is responsible for reacting when we are faced with some form of danger. For example, when a predator was about to attack one of our ancestors, the latter had to make a decision: fight or flee. Physiologically, what happens in a moment of such stress is that the brain sends a warning signal through the amygdala to the whole body, then neurotransmitter substances, among them cortisol, are produced, in order to help us survive.

To this day, this primitive component still exists within us. The only difference is that, in modern times, we do not have a predator attacking us. And unless your life is really in danger, the amygdala will alert us to situations that are perceived as threatening, but in reality they are not (my boss yelled at me, I am stuck in a traffic jam, I fought with my partner, I have many debts to pay, I see myself in the mirror and I do not like what I see, etc.).

The stress generated by these life circumstances or these damaging thoughts puts us in a "fight or flight" state, causing us to be contentious to situations, people, and even ourselves, contaminating our being physically and emotionally, to the point of becoming ill.

We live in one of the most emotionally and physically ill societies in history, and all because we have not made sense of our fears - where they come from, and what we can do to tackle them once and for all. The solution to our fears is not to flee from them, for they will continue to cast a shadow forever; but rather, to be clear on what our fears really are, and when confronted with them, to look them in the eyes with the courage to understand them, to forgive them, and to attend to them with that part of us that is ever wise and eternal: our soul!

In my own life, fear has taken over the driver's seat on many occasions and has definitely stopped me from making important decisions, subjected me to compulsive behaviors (in my case, overeating), and has compelled me to stay in undesirable comfort zones. In recent years, and through various exercises that I will share with you in this book, I have learned to give my fear a guidance role rather than one of leadership. Of course, if at any moment I am faced with a situation of life or death, fear will certainly assume its deserved position of captain.

As you will soon discover, we cannot live without fear, since it is what keeps us alive. Let´s call it the *sense of survival*. It plays a very important role in our existence, yet it becomes present in so many untimely moments, that we must make it our task not to believe in the misleading ideas it brings to our reality, such as feelings of envy, jealousy, incompetence, negativity, victimization, sabotage, not being enough, fear of failure, guilt, shame and the conviction that an external element will fill internal voids.

COMFORT ZONE VS. UNCERTAINTY

"Paola, I really want to change but it is so difficult, I am not ready."

If I had a dollar every time someone told me a version of the above statement, I would be a rich woman. We believe that being ready means "when I am not afraid to leave the comfort zone." Well, I have news for you: Very few people wake up one day feeling they are no longer fearful, and therefore, ready to surrender to the unknown. Even those brave knights and heroes from the history books have been scared, and I can assure you, that on the day of the battle they did not wake up saying, "Today I am ready and not afraid to die."

The blessed comfort zone - so referred to by many of us – can be a lethal trap that can steer us to live a lifetime of incongruity, unfulfilled dreams.

So why is the comfort zone so attractive despite its clear negative connotation?

We humans have learned that the worst thing that can happen to us is to be in a state of uncertainty. We must always know how, where, and when, and if these variables cannot be answered, our primitive fear is triggered and we prefer to stay on the shore, even when we know that the island is going up in flames. In other words, we prefer to burn in the fire rather than to jump into the high seas to find other lands.

Sound familiar?

Did you know that from zero to eighteen months of life is the time in which we create the most neurological connections? In fact, we develop more during that time than we develop from eighteen months to a hundred years. Incredible, isn't it?

The reasons are plenty, but the most fascinating one is that a child, with no knowledge, is in complete uncertainty, at the mercy of his/her parents or caregivers who teach him/her, and while trusting, in complete uncertainty, his brain is alert, learning every detail of his/her environment. The same happens to us as we get older. We hope that a crisis that unleashes uncertainty will affect us in order to find that state of faith in the unknown. Albert Einstein said so in his definition of crisis:

"Do not pretend that things will change if we always do the same. The crisis is the best blessing that can happen to people and countries, because the crisis brings progress. Creativity is born from the distress, as the day is born from the dark night. It is in crisis that invention, discovery and large strategies are born. Whoever overcomes crisis, outdoes himself without being overcome".

I agree with the above definition but would add the following: we should not wait until the crisis arises to welcome uncertainty.

Learning to surrender with faith to each moment, allowing the unknown to manifest is one of the best ways to stimulate the wisdom that lies within us.

WHAT IS THE WORST THAT CAN HAPPEN?

The ship is safest when it is in port, but that's not what ships were built for.
PAULO COELHO

When I first began my coaching training, the teacher asked us to practice with someone we already knew. I applied coaching to my family, as they were excited about my new career. My mother was one of them. She had a "stable" job but felt unfulfilled; she experienced harassment in the workplace and extremely long workdays. It was too much. Even with all these struggles, because of her positive attitude, she managed to survive that employment.

When we began with the coaching sessions, I asked her about all the areas in her life and discovered that her work stood out in each of area. I followed by asking her, "What are the reasons that stop you from leaving your current work?" She said, "I cannot quit. I have too many financial commitments and we cannot live on your father's salary alone. I then said, "Are you sure?".

You see, we humans have certain beliefs that were imposed or are a remnant of past experiences. Rarely do we stop to wonder if what we believe is the truth or only a perception of it.

It was then that we went on to analyze ways to make this possible. We started by assessing: What expenses can be trimmed down? What else can you do? What kind of skills do you have that can open doors in another company or perhaps consulting work?

We began to shed light during the assessment, but we could not stop there. I had to ask her the million dollar question: **what is the worst that can happen if you quit?**

Once I asked her, she immediately told me: I would not be able to pay my financial commitments as I would not have a monthly income. We continued:

—What is the worst that can happen if you cannot pay your financial commitments?

—That I burden your father too much with debts.

—And, what is the worst that can happen if you burden my father too much financially?

—That we could have problems with banks.

—What is the worst that can happen if you have problems with banks?

—That we lose assets because of our troubles.

—And, what is the worst that can happen if you lose assets?

—That we have no place to live and have to live on the streets.

—And, what is the worst that can happen if you live on the streets?

—We will be cold and hungry.

—And, what is the worst that can happen under such a situation?

—We will die!

EUREKA! Fear shows us that the worst scenario is DEATH! Thus, you must remain in anguish, killing yourself gradually, but not as quickly as the previous setting that would hypothetically kill you.

We delved deeper, analyzing all the scenarios:

Scenario 1: To burden someone too much.

Question 1: Have you thought about your monthly expenses, and how you could reduce them?

Answer: Well, by not working means I do not have to pay a maid to clean the house, which would be a big savings.

Question 2: With said clarity concerning expenses versus income, could you suggest the idea to your husband (my father in this case)?

Answer: Yes, I am sure he would understand me. He sees how tired and ill I am, he has told me more than once to resign.

Question 3: Your husband has businesses, could you help him?

Answer: Yes! That is true, with my management skills, I could help him get organized, and I am more assertive with employees than he his, which could help to keep money from being wasted. In addition, there are several properties that I can help him sell. Also, if I quit, I will receive some income that will give me time to settle down.

"Ahhh!," she sighed, and told me: **I feel excited, afraid, but inspired. I cannot wait to leave that job**.

I want to tell you that this conversation was enough for her to resign, but it took a few more coaching sessions, and a couple of setbacks in her workplace, which in the end were gifts from the Universe re-confirming the journey she had to take.

This does not all happen overnight. There was a lot of fear in the early phase of her transformation. Three months later, she quit her job and today she would be first to tell you that, at fifty-five, she has never been happier. Nowadays, she is willing to share her story and always begins by asking the question that changed her life "what is the worst that can happen?"

What happens is that fear clouds us, it submerges us in a cave from which we are terrified of leaving, but, once we are able to climb out of it and see the light, we will never want to hide in the cave ever again.

When we actually head out from that fictional comfort zone, our brain becomes creative. You probably have already heard the phrase "necessity is the mother of inventiveness," the problem is that we do not even give ourselves the time to consider the question, much less play with the idea.

NOW IT'S YOUR TURN

What is your current situation?

What would you like to do about it? (Be very honest with yourself)

If you decide to go for it, what is the worst that can happen?

With each response to the question, "What is the worst that can happen?" ask yourself the same question again: And what is the worst that can happen if ..., do this at least five times or until you get to the root of your fear. Once you discover your reasons for staying in the comfort zone, ask yourself if they are 100% genuine, and what other ways they could be resolved. It is amazing how we believe things without even questioning them.

Now, come up with at least 20 actions that you can do to resolve, change, or improve your current situation.

It may be that you only do one or two actions, it does not matter, the important thing is to open your mind to the possibilities. Your imagination will take you places. This is the only way that extraordinary lives are built and I know that you deserve to have one.

COURAGE AND INSPIRATION

To be a warrior is not a simple matter of wishing to be one. It is rather an endless struggle that will go on to the very last moment of our lives. Nobody is born a warrior, in exactly the same way that nobody is born an average man. We make ourselves into one or the other.

CARLOS CASTAÑEDA

The word 'courage' derives from the Latin word *cour*, which means heart.

To have courage is to do things from the heart. It is like when we are very much in love, we can and will do whatever it takes to be with that person; it is the same thing with other situations in life. The motivation to actually do things is not born of logic, it is not born in our mind. That is why it is so difficult to motivate ourselves sometimes and much more so if you have to motivate yourself to be brave. Forget it! You will probably be left waiting for that day.

The new concept I want to bring to light for you is the word INSPIRATION, and it is born not from your mind but from your heart. Dr. Wayne Dyer, when referring to several of his creations, talks about how the word INSPIRED is to be "in-spirit", or in connection with yourself, with your center.

When you discover what inspires you, what makes your heart sing, then you have access to the wisdom that exists in the Universe, to ideas and to creativity, elements that will make your soul evolve.

You may say to yourself: "I do not know what inspires me." That is why I bring you several questions to reflect upon in order to help you decode the yearnings of your soul.

1. If failing were impossible, what risks would you take?

____

____

____

____

2. If money was not a concern, what would you dedicate your life to?

____

____

____

____

3. If you had to pay to dedicate your life to something (and you had all the money to do it) what would it be?

____

____

____

____

4. If tomorrow you woke up and everything you had to do had already been resolved, how would you spend your day?

____

____

____

____

5. What do you believe is your unique way of serving the world?

____

____

____

____

6. What talents do you know you have, but for some reason you have not used them for a long time or you have never nurtured them?

____

____

____

____

7. Besides time and money, what do you most desire?

____

____

____

8. What makes your heart sing?

9. What can you do for hours without realizing that time has gone by?

10. What topics or hobbies can keep you talking about them all night?

11. What have you wanted to do for a long time but are you still postponing?

12. If you were not scared, what decisions would you make in your life?

____

____

____

____

Take your time responding to these questions. Be kind to yourself if the answers do not come immediately. It may be that so far, you have been thinking mostly from your mind and not from your heart.

Breathe, listen to your heart, and trust that if your intention is to receive answers they will come clearly and at the right time.

IT IS NOT ABSENCE OF FEAR

Nothing real can be threatened.
Nothing unreal exists.
A Course in Miracles

Several months ago, I was doing a full moon ritual with one of my best friends. This ritual consisted of meditating on everything that we had to let go of emotionally in order to allow new sensations, experiences, and people to come into our lives. She had just ended a long relationship with her boyfriend. Although her decision had been well-thought out and deliberated upon with her soul, from time to time anxiety overwhelmed her. When we were both sharing what each of us wanted to let go, she said, "I want to let go of fear." We then became silent, and something in me made me wonder: is it possible to let go of fear? And it was there that I intervened and asked her: "Perhaps it is something else you must let go?" She replied: You are right, doubt is at the root of my fear. I continued to question her, "What must you do then to dismiss your doubts little by little?"

Fear simply feeds on certain thoughts and actions. For example, listening to her family and friends' doubts about her decision made her hesitate, as well as her ongoing communication with her ex-boyfriend.

It was a sincere conversation between two close friends, as we continued talking extensively on the subject of fear and concluding that the fear is not the "bad guy." We must remember that without fear we would be dead. That is why fear must exist, to actually uphold us. In this scenario, my friend was not in any danger of dying, but the illusion and anxiety causing the doubts in her head informed her amygdala that indeed she was.

Let´s not waste time on the false illusion of "getting rid of this fear" but rather search for what is fueling it, and take the necessary measures to diminish what feeds it.

I assure you that all human beings will be afraid, to some extent, until the day they die. However, what we can do is develop courage. For example, we can develop the courage to protect your space with positive elements (thoughts, people, surroundings), the courage to confront a situation and ask yourself how you can stop feeding your fear, the courage not to believe in the fear that is plaguing you, because remember that unless your life is literally in danger, all that you imagine is only an anxious illusion.

What will you gain if you change your relationship to fear?

When you see fear for what it is, you realize that all it suggests is an illusion, and I reiterate that, unless you are truly in a life-and-death situation, everything else are apprehensive ideas of possible scenarios that point to our last day on earth. Once we understand this, we can see fear for what it is: our guide. It is then that it becomes an ally. We recognize that when we are afraid, it is simply telling us, “Be cautious, take a look at all the variables.” We are told, for example, to not cross the street without looking both ways before doing so. **Fear becomes our co-pilot and not our driver**. When we become aware of its role inside of us and allow it to assist us without dominating our existence, something else happens ... COURAGE!

The brave ones are those that with courage, decided to look at the possibilities and overcome the illusions of fear. Now, they feel at ease even if the circumstances are not so comfortable, because the brave know that truth prevails and that illusion does not exist.

Let´s give ourselves the chance to develop this incredible weapon that will help us, like the Warrior, to become the heroes of our own existence, and to enjoy the fruits of our heroism.

JUST DREAM OF BEING BRAVE BY ASKING YOURSELF THE RIGHT QUESTIONS

I learned that courage was not the absence of fear, but the triumph over it. The brave man is not he who does not feel afraid, but he who conquers that fear.

NELSON MANDELA

The moment I knew that I had to make difficult decisions, such as walking away from a relationship, therefore losing the approval of others, anguish would invade every cell of my body. In spite of this, I began to allow myself to dream, in silence, without anyone noticing. This reverie was accompanied by statements such as "I know I will not do it ever. Do not worry, Paola ... but how would it be if hypothetically you did? What would my life be like if I made this decision? What would I do? I know it is not possible to do it, but what if I did do it, where would it start?"

When the answers terrified me, I would stop and ponder again. If fear was not possible at this very moment, what would I do? And so I dreamed with the promise that it was only a speculation without really having to make any decisions.

Slowly but surely, I began to mentally build certain scenarios that were not so bad, not only because I was tricking my imagination into letting go of the fear, by not necessarily requiring myself to follow up on these reveries, but also because I was asking myself the right questions.

Are you asking yourself: Why did this happen to me? What am I going to do with all this distress? How will I be able to stay like this forever?

In the words of Tony Robbins: "Lousy questions create lousy answers!" Ask yourself questions that will empower you and you will receive the same kind of answers. As I did with my mother in the previous session, ask yourself what the options are and gradually find answers that do not make you take irresponsible actions, but rather potential acts of courage.

People remain in the same situation, year after year, because they do not dare to dream, much less ask themselves what are the various possibilities that they have in their lives. Do it. Dare to dream that you could be courageous, even if at this time, it does not seem like something realistic. What if you were brave, what would happen?

Asking yourself the right questions and allowing yourself to dream will progressively open an array of possibilities for you, and once you open this door you will soon discover its greatest treasures.

WHAT IS A BELIEF?

A belief is only a thought that you keep thinking.
Abraham Hicks

You may be thinking: "Paola, what you are saying is very nice and moving but I am still terrified, I do not know why."

It is time to talk about your beliefs. If your beliefs are not in tune with your wants, then your efforts will be sabotaged repeatedly.

I once heard an analogy that I will never forget about beliefs: beliefs are like a table. The surface of the table is the belief, but for the belief to stand steady it needs four legs to support it - in this particular case, the evidence supporting the belief are the four legs. The surface of the table (the belief) and the four legs (the evidence) cannot hold themselves together if they do not have some kind of glue that bonds them, and this glue is constituted by the emotions.

We, human beings, have two reasons why we do or do not believe in something. This can be to AVOID pain, or to move toward pleasure. We believe what we believe because somehow or another there is a positive emotion that joins the evidence to the belief. It fulfills its purpose of moving away from pain or moving toward pleasure.

Where does that belief stem from? Many beliefs are instilled in us from childhood. Some are positive and some are negative. The positive ones are those such as:

"Honesty is a very treasured value"

"Stealing or killing is bad"

"You are the outcome of your decisions"

These beliefs are thoughts that were instilled in us by our parents and family, if you grew up in a family or culture where one's honesty, integrity and power were valued.

In addition, our experiences allowed us to gather certain beliefs along the way. For example, as an overweight child and teenager, I surmised the belief that to be accepted I had to be thin and pretty. This prompted me to have eating disorders during my teenage years. My romantic relationships were a disaster due to my physical insecurities. I was bullied so much because my body was not what people expected it to be, that I amassed several erroneous beliefs regarding physical appearance and the meaning of love.

We also assimilate beliefs from different situations, whether good or bad. For this reason, we are going to discover what you believe in, and little by little, replace these beliefs with ones that are more in sync with what you want for your life.

If you want to have an energetic and healthy body but you consider that your genetics are hindering you from transforming it into one, then any diet you will try will be sabotaged by that belief. If you want to fall in love but do not believe that you are worthy of being loved, then you will sabotage your relationships or potential relationships. If you want a better job or to start your own business, but you are too terrified or believe that you are not smart enough, you will keep yourself from undertaking that project or asking for that promotion. That is why I want us to do the following:

Write down your wishes, dreams and yearnings:

____

____

____

____

Write down what you believe makes it difficult or impossible to make this wish become a reality:

____

____

____

____

Are you ready?

These are your limiting beliefs.

With this exercise we determine the most obvious limiting beliefs; the deeper you dig into your self-awareness, the more you will become aware of other hidden beliefs. You must observe your responses when faced with a situation or a new idea as it arises, and with some curiosity ask yourself, what do I believe in? Knowing yourself intimately, aside from being a great privilege, will give you the respite to heal and expand yourself in ways that you never imagined you could.

Transform your belief:

Let's do these hypothetical exercises together so that you can do them later on your own:

Questions to ask yourself:

1. What is your belief?

a) "I am not smart enough or brave enough to achieve what I want."

2. What is the positive emotion that holds that belief? Why is it right to trust what you believe in? (Open your mind and your heart when responding to this question. It is not easy but I can assure you that you trust in what you believe in because somehow you have thought it to be positive.)

a) When I believe this, I remain in my comfort zone.

b) It is easier to believe this. That way, I do not look bad in front of myself or anyone else.

c) I avoid failing if I do not risk anything.

d) I do not get stressed about a new project. That way I am calmer.

3. What evidence do you have that this is true?

a) When I was a child my father called me stupid.

b) I have always been fearful of everything, from public speaking to playing certain sports.

c) In college, I was never the best student in my class.

d) Up until now in my life I have always played it very safe. I am afraid of failure.

4. What would you prefer believing in? (Use the opposite of what you're believing now.) What would you like your new belief to be?

a) I am smart and brave enough to achieve everything I set my mind to.

5. What proof do you have that indicates that this new belief is likely or true?

a) I have never failed a class in my entire life.

b) At my job I have been acknowledged for my performance on several occasions.

c) My girlfriend always acknowledges how quick I am to solve problems.

d) I traveled alone for several months and I was not afraid to do so.

6. Alright then... since your new belief is something your brain still can NOT process, we must use small intentions that you already believe and that point you toward what you truly want to believe.

Affirmation #1: My intention is to learn to recognize how I am smart and capable already.

Affirmation #2: My intention is to recognize that my courage comes from taking action, even though I am scared.

Affirmation #3: My intention is to grow every day, to go after my dreams.

Now, it's your turn, and we are going to use the same questions to change your belief:

1. What is your belief?

____

____

____

____

2. What is the positive emotion that holds that belief? Why is it right to trust what you believe in? (Open your mind and your heart when responding to this question. It is not easy but I can assure you that you trust in what you believe because somehow you have thought it to be positive.)

____

____

____

____

3. What evidence do you have that this is true?

____

____

____

____

4. What would you prefer believing in? (Use the opposite of what you're believing now.) What would you like your new belief to be?

____

____

____

____

5. Alright then... since your new belief is something your brain still can NOT process, we must use small intentions that you already believe and that point you toward what you truly want to believe.

____

____

____

____

VULNERABILITY

Vulnerability sounds like truth and feels like courage. Truth and courage aren't always comfortable, but they're never weakness.

BRENÉ BROWN

Like many people in this moralistic, perfectionist and materialistic society, I confess that I have wanted to escape such "evil" vulnerability all my life. If I would not have been born in a matriarchy (yes, I come from a matriarchy where my strong and widowed grandmother formed nine powerful and independent women), everything would have been very different. I grew up based on the belief that crying was only for extreme reasons and that vulnerability was nothing more than a weakness that had to be purged immediately.

Growing up with these beliefs, and with the media and social expectations constantly reinforcing them, I learned to do my job very well. It entailed leaving my nonconformities unexplored and urged me to immediately resolve everything by following a comfortable route that was accepted by all, and very importantly, one that would numb a bad situation in the most efficient way.

We live in a society that insists on perfection, which focuses on what other people think and say as opposed to focusing on one's heart's desires. Criticism, judgment, and lack of forgiveness on the part of others -and of ourselves as well- promote the lethal feeling of SHAME, and thanks to it, we reach for something I call **numbness.** This implies making decisions that please our limiting beliefs or those of others, despite the fact that they go against who we are and what we truly want. Situations that might cause us to want to numb our feelings because of shame might be something like: needing to ask for help when we cannot do something alone, confessing our true feelings to someone, having to say "I don't know," or "I don't actually want...," apologizing when we know we did something wrong, "failing" at something, leaving a job or a relationship, telling your parents you are choosing your own journey instead of theirs, etc. These types of situations can be so very painful to experience, but our hearts cry out for us to go in their direction.

When we numb ourselves, we feel frustrated, stressed, anxious and we decide to take refuge in certain practices with the purpose of not feeling. Among these harboring practices, the most common are: overindulging in drugs and alcohol, gossiping (by judging others to feel better about myself), staying in dysfunctional relationships that are not going anywhere, working excessively, spending compulsively, eating too much to fill voids, immersing oneself for long hours on Facebook or in front of the television, over-socializing or isolating oneself, etc., to simply not have to deal with the fact that we decided not to see ourselves for who we are.

Brené Brown defines vulnerability as "*letting ourselves be seen*", and when I read this I thought to myself, "No way, never, people will judge me!" This is precisely the problem. We believe that if others see us for who we are, they will think less of us, we will feel bad about ourselves, we will be thought of as weak, and we shall not be worthy of love. However, studies reveal just the opposite (in addition that, selectively, we cannot numb our feelings). If we numb our sadness, anxiety, uncertainty and shame, simultaneously we are numbing our happiness, authenticity, creativity, and joy for life.

To be seen for who you are may be one of the most uncomfortable things that exists, but in my case, I have learned that only when we have the courage to tell the truth (even if our voice trembles and we act with our heart's parameter of success rather than public success), we allow our soul to evolve and reap the fruits of the courage to be vulnerable, which are unconditional love, inner fulfillment, and success in every way.

IT IS NOT WEAKNESS

How is that not weakness?

"I feel much too exposed if I am seen for who I am." That was my most consistent thought when I was deliberating about this, particularly if it pertained to a romantic relationship. For instance, sometimes I would go out with a guy and I enjoyed it, but when things did not go as I expected, I felt hurt. I then thought that having these human emotions was a weakness that I had to be stronger, smile more, be smarter, be more calculated, and more balanced.

I must confess that, in my journey, I have made progress with this argument, but it took years to weaken the belief that this was foolish, and I truthfully had to reinforce my new belief that **the entire rainbow of my emotions needed be honored**. This has been quite a struggle, but here I am!

The shame in not being what I thought was a "perfect woman" tormented me relentlessly. I carried so much resentment toward myself for not accepting that despite all the reasoning in the world, I was still human; that is to say, I will make mistakes, I will feel profound emotions in situations that touch my soul. And this carries over into professional settings: It´s ok to admit that "I do not know", "I cannot" or "it is not within my scope of knowledge."

Bit by bit, and with the help of all these tools that I am offering you in this book, I have learned to honor my vulnerability, and as author Brené Brown says: "*That which makes me vulnerable, makes me strong*"

WHAT OTHERS THINK

In my first 20 years of life I was very worried about what others thought, in my second 20 years of life I did not care at all what others thought of me, and the last 20 years of my life I realized that no one was really thinking about me.

ANONYMOUS

We must separate ourselves from the good judgment of others if we want to achieve something in life. You and I know that even if we gossip about someone, that gossip will not transcend much in our lives. Each of us is dealing with his/hers own demons, dramas and insecurities. So, the next time you worry about some gossip, simply consider this: how much time do I really think about what they told me about other people? Surely a few minutes, but let's be honest, did you really think about it all day? All week? Definitely not! You had other things to deal with including your own life.

There is a poem that resonated with me deeply the day I read it:

The Man in the Arena, by Roosevelt. Below is one of the most famous and remarkable parts of the speech:

"It is not the critic who counts; not the man who points out how the strong man stumbles, or where the doer of deeds could have done them better. The credit belongs to the man who is actually in the arena, whose face is marred by dust and sweat and blood; who strives valiantly; who errs, who comes short again and again, because there is no effort without error and shortcoming; but who does actually strive to do the deeds; who knows great enthusiasms, the great devotions; who spends himself in a worthy cause; who at the best knows in the end the triumph of high achievement, and who at the worst, if he fails, at least fails while daring greatly, so that his place shall never be with those cold and timid souls who neither know victory nor defeat."

When you dare to love yourself, to honor your essence, and to give up a social principle you figured out was not for you, there will be criticism and gossip. Your courage may ignite fears and insecurities in others. In some people because they love you and do not want to see you suffer, and in others, because you are mirroring back what could be possible for them. Whatever the reason, the one who dares will be looked upon, but that, and exactly that, will indicate that you are on the right track. So go ahead, keep your head up and keep walking. When you finally overcome the winds of change, you will have inspired thousands and helped to heal the world. When you say yes to vulnerability, you say yes to your truth.

PERFECTION VS. FREEDOM

You are enough.

How many of us suffer or have suffered from the foolish desire to be perfect? When we look for perfection in how we look, how we talk, how we do things and how the world sees us, we are preparing ourselves for a sudden stint of frustration. Fear thinks that by being or rather seeming to be perfect, the world will respect us or, something even more important: the world will not hurt us. That is why we believe: "If I dream a little or do not dream at all, what little risk I can take could look perfect in the eyes of others, and if it fails, it does not matter because, I bet so little on it that it will seem insignificant." The problem is that when fear tells you that there is no "perfection" in something, may it be your partner, your body, your finances or your projects in some way or another, your value as a person is compromised.

Let me explain myself more clearly, for some perfectionism is a form of protection. It is one of the many faulty barriers that we set upon ourselves to have some form of control. What happens is that it is a mere illusion, because as human beings, perfection in this earthly realm is not possible, plus the world is designed so that uncertainty and impermanence are the only things assured in this life.

Therefore, if we look perfectionism in the eyes we can discover the following:

It is just one more illusion of fear to protect ourselves from the world.

It is a means to postpone our dreams by not having everything perfectly aligned.

It is a form of fear to find an identity: "If I do it perfectly, then I am worthy, if not, I am a failure."

Based on the above statements, I want to ask you something: do you want to be free, do you want to be at peace with yourself and do you want to make your dreams come true? If your answer is YES, then I hereby give you the magic potion that will unleash you from this curse that you picked up on your journey up to this point:

WAIVE PERFECTIONISM TODAY AND WELCOME PROGRESS.

If you focus on *how much you are progressing*, instead of *how perfect it is*, you will keep moving forward, you will have less stress, and things in your life will flow accordingly.

Exercise:

Make a list of the ways in which you have been or are a perfectionist.

____

____

____

____

____

____

Now, answer this question:

Thanks to perfectionism, what have I stopped doing? Thanks to perfectionism, what has frustrated or disappointed me?

____

____

____

____

____

____

Then, make a list of all the things you would like to start doing, continue doing or stop doing and once achieved, will make you feel that you have taken at least one step forward, even if it is not "perfect."

____

____

____

____

____

____

This is the way in which I started my company, without any money, no chance of getting a loan, with a single computer and enough eagerness to start my coaching business. My first steps were to post free videos on the wonderful YouTube platform. In fact, if you want to, you can access my channel and check the very first videos I posted, you will see how much of a newbie I was, how difficult it was for me to express myself fluently, the under-or over-exposure of lighting in the videos given that they were taken with my cell phone, as well as the spelling mistakes. Thousands of details that, had I considered my fear's judgment and that of many who gave me their "honest" opinions, I surely would have not gone on to do a second video. Perhaps, I would have waited to attend a public speaking course, to have the money to buy a good video camera and to pay for a good editor to do something professional. But I did not listen to my fears, and told myself: if this video is watched by a single person (even if it is my mother) and that very person is touched in a positive manner by my message, it was already worth the effort. And you know something? Three months after I started posting videos on YouTube, I received messages from people in other countries telling me how much my videos resonated with them and how my message touched them deeply in moments of adversity.

One of my favorite analogies involves the life of a mother duck and her ducklings:

Have you ever seen a duck with her ducklings? It is likely that you will find a flock of ducklings with her mother, all cluttered together and when it is time to go elsewhere, you will never see the mother duck say: *okay, let me call the roll of each one of you and then we will stand in a perfect row, number one and two come to the front of the line...* If the mother duck waited for the ducklings to stand in a row and be perfectly aligned, they would never leave. Instead, the mother duck takes her first step and seconds later her ducklings, instinctively, follow her, forming a perfect row.

If we were to imitate the mother duck's attitude, surely we would stop postponing our dreams. Undoubtedly, we would refrain ourselves from saying: “I am not ready”, “it is not the right time just yet”, “I do not have enough money”, “the children are still very young.” At the end of the day, success in your endeavors will be measured by the amount of results that you attain and not with the amount of reasons or excuses you gave to justify why you did not get things done.

ACTION: CLEAN YOUR HOUSE

I know you are a person who wants to see results, and that is why you chose to read this book. You are tired of always doing the same things over and over again and getting the same results. In the end, as Albert Einstein said, this is the definition of insanity. We are now getting to a very important part of our journey. In order to take that leap of faith, we must proceed to take a very important step: CLEANING OUR HOUSE.

The concept originates from another of my favorite analogies. Imagine that someone very important, one of the people that you most admire in the world is going to visit you and stay overnight at your home. This person is very busy and staying overnight in your house is a true honor and a golden opportunity. Imagine someone of the stature of The Dalai Lama, Nelson Mandela, Gandhi, The Pope, Martin Luther King Jr; someone you really admire. Now, how do you think this very important guest would feel if he/she came to a messy house, full of garbage and clutter lying all over the place (like that TV show "Hoarders")? Surely, he/she would knock on your door and, as soon as you open it, they would see that it is difficult to walk into your home, much less eat or sleep there for the night. Then, most likely, he/she would say something like "I will come back another time, when you are less busy."

That would not be good at all, would it?

So how would you prepare yourself for this important guest? Most likely, you would clean your house, make it smell pleasant, organize cluttered areas, maybe even take advantage of the opportunity to throw out everything that was in the way (incidentally, you realize that you have certain things that you have not used for years or that you never really liked from day one, but you still had them around). Probably, you would repair certain things that are not working, you would go buy food as well as prepare some delicious dishes. Upon arrival, your guest would feel welcomed, at home, and would gracefully share with you some unforgettable moments.

Just as in the example above, that is how the Universe works with our dreams. You ask it to send you opportunities, blessings, healing, peace, happiness, money and love. Chances are that when they knock on your door, you may not even hear them because you are too busy stockpiling thoughts that mess up your mind. These are negative thoughts such as "I am not deserving," "I am not enough," "Life is good only for some people," or maybe you do have the door open but when you try to go inside you see that the walkway is obstructed with grudges, drama, illness, sadness, scarcity, discouragement, unhealthy habits, little movement, etc.

Consequently, these dreams are forced to wait outside, waiting until "the host" begins to clean the house allowing them to be able to enter and stay. If your dreams do not feel welcomed, they are so polite that they would rather wait than force their entry into your life.

Look, what I am saying is that *they are waiting*. How many of us, because we are disorganized and distracted, lose or sabotage opportunities and believe that because we spoil them, we will never be given the opportunity again? I just want to say that excluding yourself because of fear and resistance is not an eternal outcome. Ceasing the arrival of opportunities is not possible in a Universe of unlimited possibilities.

As you clean your house, your dreams will be waiting to come in when you are ready. It is never too late to receive what belongs to you.

IT IS OKAY TO FEEL THE WAY YOU DO

How many times were we told, "You do not need to cry about that." With this statement our relatives or friends were expressing some resistance to our pain. Sure, when someone does not feel well it can be quite awkward to see them suffering, more so if we love them.

Yet, these experiences teach us to ignore our feelings when we are actually sensing them. "You must be strong and focus on what is important." This is one of the things I was taught. I never saw anyone in my house crying or hardly showing any negative emotion, so I learned that the honorable thing to do was always to be positive.

And I am not saying that we should praise sadness, but rather be aware that sadness is part of life, just like frustration and anger.

As I mentioned before, the contrast of emotions-colors, flavors, and temperatures is what allows us to be grateful. If you do not know about sadness, then how will you characterize a beautiful day filled with joy? We would not know how to appreciate it.

On the journey to self-love, it is very important that we honor negative feelings, cloudy days, and without promoting misery, look into its eyes and ask: What are you here to teach me?

ACCEPT

What you resist, persists.
CARL JUNG

Let´s look our emotional discomfort in the eye.

"Stop fleeing, stop numbing yourself," is what I constantly tell myself when I want to ignore the elephant in the room, as I feel it is too heavy to deal with it. So I make an appointment with my fear, whenever I see that I have some time alone and I have a face-to-face conversation with it. I observe and sense it carefully. I inhale deeply and exhale, letting it run through my body. Inhale and exhale and slowly greet it. I welcome it and give it permission to stay for a while, I know it needs to reveal itself.

It is wonderful to see that the more I let the emotion just be and exist in my life, two things happen:

1. I learn from its clear and empowering wisdom.
2. Subsequently, it dissolves.

However, when I fight my fears, I avoid them, or I numb them with external factors, such as food, drama, alcohol, procrastination, etc., two things happen:

1. Pain is perpetuated until it becomes chronic.
2. Even if the situation slips away, it arises again as if it were telling me: Here I am, yet again, and I will keep

returning until you learn the lesson that I have come to teach you.

Once you truly feel the emotion and without wanting to change it, begin to honor it by repeatedly asking it:

Where are you in my body? What do you need me to learn?

Stay there until you transform it.

That is it, just stay there!

You will soon discover that to love oneself is to do so regardless of what one feels, wants, does and is. If we want a part of us to leave, then we are rejecting ourselves, we are sending a message that we are only adequate when we are or feel good.

BE GRATEFUL

Gratitude is one of the most healing practices that there is. You cannot be negative and thankful at the same time.

Now is the time to show gratitude to this "bad" feeling, as difficult as it may seem. And you may say: Yes, but how am I supposed to feel grateful while facing a loss of a loved one. I do not want you to arrive at this point if you have not already done the steps mentioned above, and sometimes it takes more than once to be ready for this next phase.

Do it when you are ready. The more you practice breathing and connecting with your heart, the more you know when it is time. There is no need to rush, but arriving at this point will give you peace. When you are ready, and even if you continue with that pain in the middle of your chest, say thank you, thank you for being here, thank you for all the teachings you have brought me, and thank you because I know you are expanding my existence, my possibilities.

Everything in this life happens for us, for our well-being, and never against us. We live in a friendly Universe and if our soul allowed for this assignment (challenge, crisis, chaos) to occur, it is because something is about to emerge, to be born within us that will allow us to evolve to a yet unknown level.

In my own life, when something comes about that is not very pleasant, my gratitude goes something like this:

"Thank you Universe for this assignment (emotion), even though my mind still does not understand it, I open my heart to receive the lesson."

TRANSFORM

Once you are grateful, it is time to transform.

Remember that everything happens for us, for our well-being, and never against us. It is time to use your emotions in favor of your self-growth so with this in mind I would like to present some questions that I learned to ask myself through the teachings of Reverend Michael Beckwith and his course “The Answer is You”.

Connect with your emotions and ask yourself:

If this situation were never to change, what quality would have to emerge within me in order to find peace in the midst of the chaos?

What habits am I aware now that I must let go of in my life?

What qualities and skills do I already have that can help me at this time?

These questions have transformed my life.

At the start of 2016, I had the opportunity to receive this training course. Nowadays I teach this class in a wellness center in my country, Costa Rica, and I have witnessed over and over again how these questions create miracles in people.

To transform an emotion or a situation we need to ask empowering questions, these questions will help us to find the answers within us and turn that emotion or crisis into an opportunity.

Take a few minutes, breathe, and ask yourself these questions in your head.

Wait for your intuition to dictate the answers and once you have them, write them down. Remember that writing is powerful!

GET MOVING

As part of my recipe to deal with emotions, an essential ingredient is movement. Emotions are energy in motion and when they become trapped in our body, they need to move around so they may follow their course.

In their research, the Mayo Clinic Health Letter has concluded that sitting for a long time or long bouts of inactivity are as bad as smoking.

That is why we must learn to move, and not only with the intention of improving our physical health, but because it is crucial in transforming our emotions. And I am not just referring to negative emotions, but also positive ones. In fact, when you are feeling something positive and nice, enhance that emotion, amplify it and make it more magnetic through movement. You will increase your energetic field and find answers where you had never found them before. I talk with so many of my clients and they confide in me: "Paola, I think and think about this and I just cannot find a solution." My response to them is: STOP THINKING SO MUCH AND START TAKING ACTION.

In truth, sometimes the action may not even be related to the problem or situation you are going through, but physically you must take action. So, go for a walk as soon as you feel like you are experiencing a negative emotion, enroll in a dance class, listen to music, go jogging, release that emotion through dance. Emotions are also physical experiences, so get your body moving and you will see how your feelings will move to the rhythm.

LEARN AND GROW

By this time, you have put your feelings in motion. Now, it is time to learn and grow.

To learn, we need for our consciousness to be in a high vibration level, so I recommend following the aforementioned steps:

Accept.
Be grateful.
Transform.
Get moving.

These steps create a space to reach the last learning phase: growth. If we are not growing or progressing, then we really are not taking advantage of the great school that is Life. Many people despair, wondering: but what is my purpose in life? To which I like to answer: your purpose is to be genuinely happy. Be mindful, however, as happiness does not necessarily mean you have huge smile on your face all the time, but rather, as Aristotle says, to be happy is when what I do and with whom I surround myself promotes self-growth, to become the best version of myself.

What I want to tell you is that sometimes we need challenges to grow. We have fallen into the trap of longing for a "perfect" life with no challenges to attain happiness. Imagine a life without trials. It would be quite boring and our brains, as well as our emotional development, would mature very poorly, because no effort would be required.

Once we accept that the challenges or hardships we experience are a gift, a divine lesson, then we can move on to this learning phase. For this, I bring forward more questions:

What was or is good about this situation?

What actions do I now understand that I must take in order to move forward?

Based on my new-found knowledge, what can I do better next time?

CHAPTER III

INTEGRATION

Who Are You?

Who am I? Now that is the question of all questions that can lead us to doubt or respond ambiguously. I, myself, can say: I am Paola, I am a woman, I am Costa Rican and I am a coach. But if you really notice, I am not telling you who I truly am, but rather what is my name, gender, nationality, and profession, which, despite being parts of me, are not who I am entirely.

Let´s take a look at these hypothetical scenarios to illustrate to you that I am not really who I say I am above.

If for some reason I have to change my name or nationality, or if, for some motive, I have to give up my citizenship and adopt another one, would I stop being who I am? And if, for some rationale, I no longer practice my coaching profession, then, would I cease to be who I am?

So, to the question *Who am I*? We must add: Who am I without the usual characteristics that you are accustomed to placing after the "I am."

Maybe you are love, maybe you are joy, maybe you are abundance.

So, who are you?

As we grow up, we adopt a personality that is influenced by our surroundings and by our experiences. We believe that we must be a certain way to be loved, accepted and approved by others, and for that reason, we take on labels that identify us with our being.

In this section, I want to challenge you to question yourself beyond what you think you are and discover which parts pertain to your essence and what other parts are only masks that you have embraced over time. For this purpose, the following is an exercise I learned some time ago, from Mr. Jairek Robbins and his book *Live It!: Achieve Success by Living with Purpose.* It consists of six questions:

1. When you were a child, who did you most want love from - not who you got the most love from - but who you wanted love from most?

In my particular case, it was the approval of my family and my schoolmates.

2. What did you have to be (in your mind's perception) for the person to give you the love you wanted?

I had to look my best, not be too emotional, and be a good person.

3. What could you NEVER be, because you knew (in your mind's perception, or in reality) the person would immediately take their love away from you?

I could never look disheveled, be shy, or be very sentimental.

4. Who are you today?
I am independent and strong, I am always looking for ways to be healthy, empathetic, jovial, brave, adventurous.

5. What should you add or remove to become the most authentic version of yourself?

Add: the courage to be transparent in my vulnerability and gentleness.

Remove: showing false strength and being too hard on myself.

6. What do I need to do more and what do I need to do less of in order to live the life of my dreams?

Do more: always honor my emotions, be strong in my vulnerability, continue to be courageous to take risks and make radical changes.

Do less: show false strength, want to impress those who cause me some form of threat. Allow myself to observe and not always actively participate in everything.

7. Which values would you like to guide your life then?

Femininity, collaboration, gentleness, love, joy, vitality, peace, creative expression, humility, courage, truth, honesty, beauty, fun, compassion, and kindness.

Alright then, how about we place the above values after I AM.

I am creativity.
I am femininity.
I am collaboration.
I am gentleness.
I am love.
I am joy.

Now, it is your turn:

1. When you were a child, who did you most want love from-not who you got the most love from-but who you wanted love from most?

____

____

____

____

2. What did you have to be (in your mind's perception) for the person to give you the love you wanted?

____

____

____

____

3. Who could you NEVER be, because you knew (in your mind's perception, or in reality) the person would immediately take their love away from you?

____

____

____

____

4. Who are you today?

____

____

____

____

5. What should you add or remove to become the most authentic version of yourself? What do I need to do more and what do I need to do less of these lists in order to live the life of my dreams?

____

____

____

____

6. Which values would you like to guide your life then?

____

____

____

____

7. Who are you?

____

____

____

ENERGY

Energy is not created or destroyed, it is only transformed.
ANTOINE-LAURENT DE LAVOISIER

Now that you know who you are, who you are not, what you want to remove and what you want to add, it is time to talk about something else, about *what* you are, and that is ENERGY. We are energetic beings, with trillions of vibrating energy cells that are constantly being transformed in our body.

Hard to believe, right? But that is how it is, that is reality.

Let's do this exercise:

Right there, where you are, put your two hands together in prayer position and now begin to rub them against each other, rub your hands until you feel some heat in the middle of both of them. Now, separate your hands and put one palm in front of the other, as if you were holding an invisible ball in the middle of them. Open and close your hands without joining them and just feel how this energy ball shrinks and expands.

The reason why I am asking you to do this exercise is because sometimes it is very difficult for the mind to understand about energy and vibrations. That is why I want to give your mind a little test, or in other words, a "see to believe" demonstration; however, in this case it is rather a "feel to believe" experiment.

In doing this exercise, all we did was activate the vibration of our hands' cells through friction, which allows us to understand that, just like our hands, our whole body vibrates according to the level of energy that rubs our cells together.

Let me explain myself better. Everything in this Universe is made up of energy that vibrates at different frequencies. This includes all objects and living things, including you and me. In the case of Human Beings, we can also call this energy "Life" or "Force" or "Life Force", whatever way you wish to call it. That which lives within you, what keeps you on this planet, we can call it ENERGY.

That is why when I say I AM, and I do not put any adjective or qualifier before or after it, I remain in the AM. That BEING, that part that has no name, no occupation, no economic nor marital status, that unit that we can also call ENERGY: the source, the vibration, the life.

How is this described?

Well, it is complicated to describe or explain because it goes well beyond the intellect. This energy is palpable. Energy and its vibrations operate in high and low vibrations. Low vibrations in humans are associated with thoughts, words and actions of defeat, scarcity, frustration, pain, laziness, heartbreak, illness; while high vibrations are related to thoughts, words and actions of empowerment, love, strength, opportunities, abundance, health.

How about we do another practice:

Think about an unpleasant moment in your life. A moment where you would have given anything to not be in your shoes.

Close your eyes and remember. What happened? Who was involved? What happened that hurt you so much?

Ready?

How do you feel?

Sad, angry, melancholic.

How does your body feel? Stressed, lacking energy?

If I would have performed a test of strength on you while you are in those thoughts, most likely you would have seen how your body loses strength and energy.

Let´s do this other exercise:

Think about one of the most beautiful moments of your life. A moment where you knew that you did not need anything else and did not want to be in any other place but there.

Ready!

Close your eyes, breathe in the moment, recreate it, taste it, love it as if you were reliving it again.

How do you feel?

If your mind did not interrupt you, you are probably feeling strong, centered, content. Meaning that thanks to the brain impulses your thoughts produced, your cells were charged with a high vibration.

A few years ago, when I was running a lot, something would happened that proves this.

When I had empowering and happy thoughts of nice memories or of visualizations about my dreams, I ran faster, time went by quicker and livelier. But when I thought of a sad, embarrassing or guilty moment, I immediately felt a terrible weight in my body, to the point that sometimes I stopped running, as if a force closed in on me and said, “There is no more energy to run.”

I am telling you this because I need you to understand **the power that we have when we take care of this energy**, when we pay attention to the vibration of our being, of this infinite part that is not created or destroyed, but is capable of being transformed.

YOUR BEST ALLY

Energy is your best ally.

When we vibrate with high energy frequency, or in other words, when our thoughts and emotions are positive, loving, abundant and full of possibilities, we are creating a state of being so magnetic and powerful that, when it comes to creating and introducing ourselves to the world, we become light.

When we spend some time without having a romantic relationship and unexpectedly we fall in love with someone and think to ourselves: "How strange, now that I am going out with someone I feel more attractive and I am getting many interested looks." The reason for this is not that we have become more attractive or charismatic, the motive is that falling in love is an energy that vibrates very high and allows us to shine brighter under a new light that was previously dimmed. That is why we have a responsibility to take care of our energy so we can present ourselves and do our best work in the world.

In my personal case, it is very evident how the quality of my work changes as well as the way I relate to others when I am with a lower and denser energy. I have learned that it is important to treat my energy as my most valuable asset, and although many would say it has to do with time, I am convinced that is not so, because time is relative. Einstein explained this in his theory of relativity that time is relative to the state of the observer. I am not a physicist but I will explain this better with an analogy that exemplifies it well:

If at this very moment you put your thumb on a hot dish for a minute, I am sure it would be the longest minute of your life. In matters of the heart, when you are dating someone you love very much, one minute can be like a fleeting second.

What is the difference in this particular example? One minute of pain is longer than one minute of love? As I mentioned you before, us human beings do things for two reasons: to escape from pain or to achieve pleasure or well-being.

Now lets analyze what this has to do with your energy.

The energy that we carry with us when we find ourselves in lethargic states of frustration, pain, anger, sadness, dismay, envy, fatigue, stress, revenge and misery is an energy that travels slowly and densely through us.

Just try and complete a project efficiently when you are in an energy state like the one described above. You will see how something that can take you a few hours can last up to weeks to be finished. Or try to resolve a situation or carry an effective conversation with someone when you are experiencing low energy levels and you will see how difficult it is to access the wise and intelligent part of your being.

On the other hand, what happens when you are excited, cheerful, inspired, rested, abundant, compassionate, grateful and loving? Suddenly, we are swifter in finishing our tasks, we find clear answers to complicated situations, we feel that we can undertake our responsibilities and, additionally, have enough time to help others.

Let me continue with the example of two people who recently fell in love. They can talk for hours until dawn and suddenly the world becomes a friendlier and abundant place. I am not telling you that you have to wait to fall in love with someone to feel this way. What I want to say is that through my own experience and that of my clients, when we access the powerful and creative energy that is permeated by positive emotions, we are unstoppable, magnetic, and abundant.

So, how can we care for and optimize our energy?

Let me ask you this question first. Have you already put in practice Chapters I and II? These two chapters are great magnetic energy triggers, because they align us and they set forth our coherence with who we are.

If you are not living the life that you want and additionally, you are not implementing any action to improve your internal situation, any suggestion that I give to help you optimize your energy will not have a significant impact. I am not saying it will not have an effect, but it will be more difficult.

Many of my clients are leaders or entrepreneurs who have many concerns, stress, and often disregard their personal relationships and health, causing terrible bouts of INSOMNIA to make matters worse. They tell me: "Paola, I go to bed at midnight and by four in the morning I am awake" or "I go to bed and fall asleep for the first hours of the night but by three in the morning I am already awake. My brain continues working to try and resolve all the problems I left behind in my office."

Does this sound familiar?

One of the secrets to having an energy that gives you super powers, is to sleep at least an average of seven to eight uninterrupted hours per night. This varies depending on your body, but in general this is quite accurate.

I could tell you that you have to sleep more, but how will you if your mind does not shut up or it wakes you up at dawn trying to resolve everything in the world from your pillow? That is why it is necessary, first, to clean your house of worries and inconsistencies that are causing your nervous system to be upset and your mind to race like a wild horse without any brakes. Hence, I do hope that you are putting in practice the actions mentioned in Chapters I and II, so we can move on to the integration phase and apply important practices to elevate your energy.

KNOW, RESPECT AND TAKE CARE OF YOUR ENERGY

It is important to be aware of our energy so we can respect and care for it.

What do I mean by this? It is essential to observe our emotions in light of the different activities that we partake in during the day.

This will serve as a guide to best discover two things:

1. How my energy behaves during the day.

2. What activities, during the day, rob my energy and why.

If I go back to those moments in which I know that I am disconnected from myself and I am not caring for my energy level, these are my answers:

Q: From one to ten, how are my energy levels? One being that my energy level is very poor and ten being that I feel incredibly energetic.

A: A five: "I have been tired lately.

Q:"How do you feel when you get up in the morning?

A: I feel tired, like I want to keep on sleeping.

Q: When you get up, do you need coffee to wake you up?

A: Yes, if I do not have my morning coffee, I am unable to complete my daily tasks.

Q: How do you feel, from one to ten, after breakfast, lunch, and dinner?

A: After breakfast: between seven and eight
After lunch: a five
After dinner: a seven

Q: On weekends, how are your energy levels?

A: I feel better, but I wish I could get more sleep.

A: Do you feel that in some activities you have more energy than in others? If so, indicate which ones.

IT GIVES ME ENERGY	IT ROBS MY ENERGY
When I am giving a lecture, a coaching session or attending a meeting.	When I have to sit for long hours at a time in front of the computer.
When I sleep well.	When I sleep less than seven hours.
When I exercise in the morning.	When I drink alcohol.
When I eat healthy.	When I say yes to situations, people, or projects that I originally should have said no to.
When I practice gratitude.	When I eat processed foods.
When I dance, surf or practice any of my hobbies.	
When I listen to upbeat music.	

Now it's your turn:

From one to ten, how are your energy levels? One being that your energy level is very poor and ten being that you feel incredibly energetic.

From one to ten, how do you feel when you get up in the morning?

When you get up, do you need coffee to wake you up?

From one to ten, how do you feel after breakfast, after lunch, and after dinner?

On weekends, how are your energy levels?

Do you feel that in some activities you have more energy than in others? If so, indicate which ones.

What situations rob your energy levels?

IT GIVES ME ENERGY	IT ROBS MY ENERGY

It is important to be aware of our energy to be able to know what it is asking from us and in many instances, what it is telling us or alerting us about. It may be informing us that we should not follow a certain path, depending on how we feel energetically when we think about it. Or perhaps it may be revealing to us that we may have some vitamin or mineral deficiency in our body or possibly be warning us of the presence of a disease. Our energy speaks to us just like our emotions, in fact they go hand in hand and are here to help us.

How do we honor it? My answer to this is that we learn to listen carefully and proceed to use our best judgment to make us feel good.

We live in a workaholic society that ignores how it may affect our body and our emotions. I once heard someone say that we can measure our health based on how much energy we have. It makes sense, right? If our body becomes sick, the first thing it does to defend itself is to use up all of our energy to heal. The problem is that we spend a lifetime overlooking this and "helping ourselves" or energizing ourselves in the most harmful ways: large amounts of coffee or energy drinks (which should be illegal), sometimes pills, and in some cases, illicit drugs to be able to stay alert. The outcome is that it leaves us feeling anxious, depressed, with exhausted adrenal glands and diseases that eventually become chronic.

Let´s place our energy as an object that must be honored. The obedience that we must exert to our energy, when respected, is because the qualities, situations and circumstances that it brings, determines our life's success. When we go against our energy, what it tells us is definitely something else: we offend and abuse our body, we injure it. Would you agree that it deserves respect? Learning to respect it is a process, it is a discipline, but I assure you that it is an act of self-love so deep that you will not feel an obligation, but rather a pleasure to serve it. In the end, this is why we do things, to distance ourselves from pain or go in the direction of pleasure.

How can we care for our energy?

First, we need to see it for what it is: our source of life! We are energy, and by denying it, we deny ourselves. By loving it, we love ourselves. I know that sometimes it is easier to look outward first, before internalizing, so I want us to do the following practice together.

Think about the attributes that the person you love must have or that you would like him/her to have (if he/she does not have them already).

In my case, I can say that this special person must be: kind, friendly, fun, adventurous, loving, interesting, passionate, strong, compassionate and honest.

Now I can take those characteristics and turn these into questions like:

Am I kind to my energy?
Am I friendly with myself?
Am I fun when it comes to taking care of my energy?

Am I adventurous in finding ways to discover myself and see what works for me?

Am I loving when it comes to caring for my energy?

Am I passionate when it comes to defending my well-being?

Am I strong enough to set myself limits and set boundaries to others in order to care for my energy?

Am I compassionate when it comes to seeing what changes I need to make?

Am I honest when making decisions in order to feel better?

I am going to suggest to you several things that I do to take care of my energy. I want you to know that what works for me may not necessarily work for you. So discover for yourself, explore the possibilities and fall in love with a new lifestyle that provides you with everything that you are looking for.

So then, let´s proceed to the four most important suggestions I wish to share with you:

SLEEP: In her book, *Thrive*, Arianna Huffington of The Huffington Post, devotes a whole chapter to sleep. She refers to what I consider to be a notable phrase that says "sleep your way to success." In her book, she discloses a study performed at Harvard University, which indicates that a person who sleeps 4-5 hours a day for a week or is sleep deprived for 24 hours straight triggers a deterioration in their blood equivalent to having a blood alcohol level of 0.05 percent.

This implies that when we are not sleeping enough, not only are we more emotional and less alert, but we are in a state of drunkenness. I have witnessed this when I have traveled long distances and I have not been able to sleep well, or for some reason, I have gone more than twenty-four hours without sleeping. There is a feeling of heaviness, awkwardness, you cannot speak coherently. I end up drinking coffee to force my adrenal glands to produce energy and an anxious energy or what I call a "false energy" overcomes me.

In her book Arianna suggests several things; however, one of my favorites is to set an alarm to go to sleep and in doing so you will develop an awareness that it is equally important to go to sleep early in order to fulfill your hours of sleep and repair your cells all night as it is to get up early in order to meet your responsibilities. By going to sleep early your brain will get the rest it needs to function better and to have a better memory. If you notice, this is part of the commitment we have with ourselves, our families and our duties. If we carry on almost "drunk" because we are not sleeping properly, then what kind of integrity and responsibility are we displaying?

GET MOVING: I was once participating in a conversation about the power of exercise for our bodies and minds. One of the people in the conversation said,

"A gentleman once explained this to me so clearly that I no longer had any doubts. He told me that when you do not exercise, your mind tends to take a situation and transform it into something big. In contrast, when you exercise, situations tend to remain small or very small."

People who exercise have happier brains, with less stress and anxiety. Many studies suggest that parts of the brain that control thinking and memory are greater in volume in people who exercise compared with those who do not. These areas, when we are in good shape, enable us to be people who can respond to the challenges of life more clearly and proactively. When we exercise, we transform our energy into creative energy and possibilities. Our mind suffers most when we do not have enough blood and oxygen to irrigate it. We must help it to function as if we were watering a beautiful plant, the plant of life.

Let´s do ourselves a favor and begin to make "movement" a requirement as important as eating or sleeping. If you do not like going to the gym, then walk, dance, bike. If you consider that you do not have much time, then go for a thirty-minute walk during your lunch break.

In his book, *The 4-Hour Workweek*, Tim Ferriss states, "A lack of time is a lack of priorities." Imagine that tomorrow someone puts a gun to your head and tells you: *if you do not start exercising every day I will kill you.* Would exercise become a priority, or not? No one is putting a gun to our head, but somehow or another we are putting it to ourselves by leading sedentary lives.

BE GRATEFUL: Did you know that negative thoughts are able to intoxicate our body to the point of making us sick? What happens to a sick body? The body needs to heal because it is magnificent and it wants to keep us alive for as much as it can in this world. When it tries to heal itself, it uses all the energy it has to restore itself, leaving you exhausted.

Many clients have told me: "Paola, I sleep well but it seems as if I am not rested. I am not that busy at work, but there are situations that have me thinking. I do not exercise and I do not complete the tasks that I have to do very well because I always feel as if I am exhausted. "

What do you think is the most important thing I note from this? "There are situations that have me thinking." Assuming that this is a mind without much emotional discipline, then surely thinking of "the situation" comes in the form of negative thoughts such as:

"It always happens to me."

"I hate this person."

"I hate being this way."

"I hate this situation."

"I cannot do that."

"I am not enough."

"They talk about me ..."

"I cannot believe they mistreat me in this way."

"Life is so hard."

"I will never be able to get out of this."

...among thousands of other things that our mind says.

Notice how, in the previous paragraph, I referred to "an undisciplined mind." When our minds run aimless like a wild horse, it will run around without any direction, leaving you exhausted from all the running and from fear. One of the most powerful disciplines I have discovered in recent years is the power of gratitude. You will see, when we are thankful, we raise our energy because we connect with abundance. A frightened and uncontrolled mind tends to seek the "worst case scenario" so that we can somehow control, manipulate and change the situation with our mind and with our thinking. Sounds crazy, right? Our mind needs light to remove darkness from thoughts of scarcity. This light is called gratitude. You will realize that when you are grateful, you will not be able to have all those limiting thoughts at once. Simply, when there is light there is no darkness, they do not coexist in the same place. One eliminates the other.

How do you want to live?

I hope your answer is "to live in the light." So, let´s learn how to turn on that light, with this wonderful tool.

How am I so convinced that this works? Because of the wonderful miracles I have witnessed in using its power. Everything I have told you in this book has already been proven to me. And I can provide you with many testimonies.

One of them happened as I was going to visit my parents in the city one day. I was at my lowest point financially, so, wanting to save money, I decided to go by bus. Along the way, I was thinking, "I have no money, what am I going to do? Besides, I feel bad today, I have eaten badly, I can see it in the fit of my clothes, surely my body is full of stress and I am getting fat, I am a fraud, I do not even know why I am a life coach, this is not going to work. At that moment, I caught my mind in action, in rebellion and told myself: I don´t accept this, let´s be grateful. So I started to affirm:

"I am grateful for this moment of uncertainty because it teaches me to trust."

"I thank my country that has a good transportation system that allows me to travel comfortably."

"I am grateful for my mother who is waiting for me at the bus terminal. Aww, my Mom! I am so grateful for how incredibly loving she is."

"I am grateful for my body's discomfort, because it helps me to love myself unconditionally."

"I appreciate the temporary money shortage, because this allows me to seek new ways to generate resources."

"I am grateful to have a computer, a cell phone and Internet access, since they are tools that indicate that I am one of the few privileged people in the world who have access to these luxuries, and this already makes me abundant."

"I am grateful for remembering this exercise and having the courage to resort to it when it would be easier to be miserable."

And so I continued, until, little by little, I began to feel my energy being transformed into a high and rapid energy. My situation was not critical, it was complicated, but by seeing everything I was and already had, I saw the tools I needed to overcome any obstacle. I have turned to this exercise in the midst of an illness, in complicated work situations and in breakups.

Now it is your turn.

I recommend that if you can write it down, do so, if you are alone and do not want to write it down, then say it out loud, and if you feel comfortable and you are with someone, share it with that person. Many people have a diary where every night, before bedtime, they write down the reasons for which they are grateful. This practice is so powerful that, days after that trip, I was inspired to write this poem:

I wait for better days, days when shame does not fill my bones with bitterness, where I am freer than my mind.

I know that life is always good to me, and even if there are bad days I will always remember that there are daybreaks filled with new possibilities.

I hope that we always have a smiling soul to love, to laugh, and that even if the day is gray and the soul is tired, remember that sometimes we do not win and when, paradoxically, that happens, we may be winning a lot.

I want to jump into the abyss, I want to escape to that day where everything will be well. That day where I sing in the morning and where so many butterflies dance in my stomach.

That day is today.

Today, although hard, we have done well, we have done the best we can, today we deserve vivid colors and sweet flavors.

Today we love life even if darkness is invading this day.

Be thankful.

Thank the torture that reminds us of the pain in others who often dance this dense rhythm of sadness. It is not fair, it is not fair! They say, but they do not know that justice dresses up in different disguises.

Sometimes what is just and necessary is to submerge ourselves there for a moment, in neglect, in our own rejection, so that when we remember it, we can be grateful for that day and with a greater desire, operas of happy birds will smile and share the good news about to arrive.

That day belongs to us!

We are responsible for our fury, as much as our joy, that is why we must survive, we must fall a thousand times and underfeed the ego when we realize that we can get up.

That fragile, foolish ego that swells when you distract yourself.

Today it will not dominate, nor tomorrow. Today we will get up to work only for the days of light, days of gratitude.

Today I expect many beautiful mornings and protective moons.

Today we are free. I hope we do not forget it.

EAT LIVING FOOD: My colleague and friend, Catalina Vargas of www.Cataploom.com, has been a great influence on my eating habits. She suggests in her talks that the most important thing about food is not to count how many calories or carbohydrates a product has, but to focus on the food itself and its nutrients.

The difference between a food and a product is simple: a product is anything that has a long-term expiration date and has more than one ingredient on its label. On the other hand, a food is the opposite. It is something that can be easily damaged so you have to eat it when it is fresh and only has one ingredient. In summary, foods are fruits, vegetables, grains, legumes and white and red meats. The above foods are of great benefit to our energy as they provide many nutrients, vitamins and minerals, helping our body to recover and strengthen itself. Additionally, among foods there is a further classification: living/raw foods or cooked foods. Raw foods are foods that come from the ground and do not go through a cooking process. These foods, in addition to having great nutritional content, have enzymes that help in your digestion.

The effort and the oxygen that our digestion requires, uses a lot of our energy. That is why when you eat a lot or eat badly, you feel tired and want to sleep afterwards. Your digestive system is undergoing a great task, leaving you without much energy to think, pay attention and do your activities. That is why, with less effort and oxygen required, less energy will be needed and you will have a stash of energy for your body to use for other activities. Furthermore, raw food is food that helps our blood to be more alkaline and non-acidic. The alkalinity of our body is key to achieve higher energy levels.

Our blood has a pH (hydrogen potential), and it measures the state of acidity, neutrality or alkalinity within it. When our body is acidic, it tends to become inflamed at the cellular level, and when there is inflammation in our body, we create an environment in which more diseases can develop. Instead, in a body in which the blood is alkaline, it is said that it is a body that is not compatible with diseases, as it has a strong immune system. We deduce that when we eat living food we have more energy.

Catalina suggests that at every meal we look to have at least 50% of our plate be filled with live food. If you find it very hard to eat raw foods, I invite you to visit her page and refer you to the green juice section. Green juices and smoothies are a great alternative to eating raw food, as it makes it easy to pack a lot of raw nutrition into each drink. A diet filled with processed products (baked goods, sweetened cereals, hydrogenated oils, dairy products, saturated fats, desserts, canned foods, fast foods, fried foods, white sugar, refined flours, etc.) is one way to guarantee having less energy and more lethargy. The brain and the nervous system also suffer a lot and leave you struggling to pay attention, to create, and to feel good.

The acronym for Standard American Diet is SAD and we know that the term "sad" is never good. If it helps, remember every time you eat non-live products, you are eating sad food that will bring sadness to your body. It is important that you put this into practice, and to achieve this, I first want you to observe what you eat for a few days.

Over the next three days, without changing anything, just pay attention to what you eat and how you feel after eating it. Once you have this covered, sit back and analyze what foods lower your energy and which ones you could substitute for healthier ones. I know that in the beginning it can be a bit difficult, especially if you do it alone. I suggest that you contact a holistic nutritionist who will know how to guide you on the right path. It is worth researching and learning more about energy supply. You will see how the benefits that you will reap will immediately reflect themselves in your energy levels, your mood and your health.

ENERGY TO CREATE, VISUALIZE

Now we are ready, we have our tools in action and I am confident that you are already getting a good night's sleep, you are moving about, you are in grateful mode and you are eating live food.

We are ready to create through visualization.

Albert Einstein said "Logic will get you from A to B. Imagination will take you everywhere."

Everything we see on a physical level was at some point in someone's imagination. That is why, in this section, I want to tell you that it is not so different with our lives.

About twelve years ago, as I was on my way to work at my first job, I said to my mother, "How nice would it be to be able to live at the beach, get up, and know that you could work on something that you are passionate about?" My mother, at the time, listened to me but did not say much. Years later she confessed what she had thought at that moment: "This girl does not know what life is about." She, being a wise mother, did not refute my comment and chose not to say much. She knew that destroying someone's dream with negativity would turn me into person with little dreams. I remember that, like any job, at the start of our lives, I knew that I would not stay there forever. I dared to daydream. I perfectly recall how I imagined my life: I would wake up in my beach house, I would surf or exercise in the morning and I had a 4x4 car for rugged roads. I did not know what I was going to do for a living, but I knew I would enjoy it very much. I knew that I wanted to live at the beach. My new job would have to be in a tourist area, near one of my favorite beaches.

So, exactly six years went by, and life had brought me to Brazil, where I got a job, having just obtained my college degree. In Brazil, I decided to live near the beach and my job was to teach English and Spanish, which I truly enjoyed and loved for the year and a half that I lived there. Once I returned to Costa Rica, I knew that my heart would be much happier if it was near the ocean, so I went to live at the beach again, and four years later I received a call to participate in a project, guess where? That's right, at the beach in the tourist area that I previously mentioned. I would be doing what I am I passionate about: Coaching and being my own boss, with my own schedule. I would be able to exercise to the rhythm of the ocean and live exactly where my much younger self, who seemed to barely know anything about the world, dreamed she would twelve years prior.

This is one of the greatest things I have manifested with the power of visualization, but I have also attracted to my life, business, people, circumstances, services, and products that when I first imagined them, my fears arose, stating: "Never, Paola, that is impossible" but, as I have learned: if my soul can dream it, then I can achieve it.

I do not want to create false illusions here, the visualization must be accompanied by a great dose of action, but when you have a great vision of what you want your life to be and you understand that a great dream is fulfilled by many small and tangible steps and you surrender to it, the creative power of the Universe will conspire to put in your path the pieces you need to play a great game.

This is what I call the co-creation process.

When I started my coaching practice, I knew that I wanted to have an online presence. It was then that I bought a program from a great coach who taught me exactly what I was looking for. Her name is Marie Forleo and her program is B-School. She was a great example of what could be achieved and I wanted to learn what she had done to manifest her success. One of her first tips was to have a great vision and also to know that this great vision needed small steps. I took the first of one of those little steps a couple of years ago. She suggested that one of the best ways to promote coaching services was through *blogging* and consistency in this task was key.

As she did, I was very interested in making video blogs instead of writing. So, on April 16, 2013 I took it upon myself to start my channel called ***Paola Castro Coaching*** and today as I write this, I can proudly say that I have more than 100 videos uploaded on my channel. These videos have attracted audiences from Mexico, the United States, Spain, Argentina, Switzerland, Chile, Peru, and many other countries. If a few years ago I had stopped to think if this was possible, all the statistics of my limited mind would have said: "NO, Paola...who are you that people would stop and watch a video of you? There is a lot of competition out there! You do not have a professional camera to do this with!" And blah blah blah ... To a certain extent, it was true what my mind would have said, but I didn't care. The experience with the videos has improved in the last years, and what before took me half a day to record, now I do in ten minutes. So you see, when we do things with vision, passion, service and consistency, the Universe answers back.

Now, why is it so important to visualize first? When we visualize we are putting ourselves in a high energetic state. Consequently, when we train our mind to create through our imagination, our actions unconsciously follow our thoughts.

Someone once said: "Worrying is like asking for what you do not want." If in our mind we are placing mental images or visualizations that represent fatalistic, discouraging, and negative outcomes, then your actions will follow that pattern of thinking, creating exactly what you did not want to happen.

From Oprah to Olympic athletes, many use this innate visualization power that we have. That is why I do not want you to waste it. Start using it TODAY!

The benefits will be incredible.

GENERATE AN ENVIRONMENT TO CREATE

You are the average of the five people you spend the most time with.
JIM ROHN

It is true that we create our own reality through a clear vision of what we want, healthy practices to keep your energy levels high, and a series of actions that lead you to achieve your goal. In turn, the Universe gets your signal that you are now ready to receive what you have been longing for.

It is important to add one more step and this is to generate an environment that will help you create. This setting can range from where you live, to how you live, and with whom you connect. This point is crucial in our ability to create. While it is true that nothing affects us unless we allow it to, inevitably, if you are in an environment with low and dense energy, and you only spend time with negative people or with those who are simply not on your same page, it will be much harder to operate at a level where you have room to expand.

This is what I call helping yourself win! How? Helping yourself win includes all the practices and habits we have discussed so far, as well as providing environments where inspiration and enthusiasm are easy to experience.

The people that surround us have great influence on us, just as we have on them. Jim Rohn could not have said it better: “We are the average of the five people we spend the most time with.” Who are these five people in your life? When my tribe is a group of people who dream big, who believe in the abundance of resources and not in their scarcity, and they can celebrate the triumphs of others (because they know that when a person wins, we all win) my life has an exponential growth curve.

Now, I am not suggesting that you cut off all your friends and family if currently these people are not a tribe that positively influences you. It is not about that, it is more about looking, intentionally, for those people we may already know, and when we speak, our conversations are open and supportive.

What happens if we do not know anyone like that? Well, I want you to make an inventory of people who have passed through your life, for example: teachers, bosses, ex-colleagues or co-workers and people you admire (yes, it may be that you only know them online).

Have you thought of anyone yet? Now, how can you approach him or her? In my case, I have my series of “experts” in the coaching field and I have contacted many of them through Facebook. True, not all answered back, but at least I showed interest and some have had the courtesy and the time to give me their opinion or advice. Besides, it does not matter if I don´t get to know them personally, they are part of the podcasts I listen to, the Facebook pages I follow, and the groups in social networks where I have found people that, although we cannot physically exchange ideas and opinions, we can relate.

What subjects are you interested in? Can you enroll yourself in a course where you will meet new people who share your same interests? Which groups on Facebook would you like to belong to? Come on, go for it. As the saying goes "If the mountain does not come to Muhammad, Muhammad goes to the mountain." There are no excuses not to accomplish this. The excuse, of course, will be set forth by your fears, but at this time, I trust that you are training your mind not to believe in the limiting illusions of fear.

Do you live in a household where your parents or relatives are negative? In a work environment where your associates are hurtful and drain your energy? Well, maybe it is time to become independent, to recalibrate your relationships, to ask for a promotion, or to change jobs. What should your next move be, based on the indications provided by your situation? I know it is not always simple to change your surroundings, and it may not happen overnight, but remember that the beginning of all transformation is to question the status quo and see what possibilities you have to change and improve. Just like as with your friends, also check your home and your office. Is what you see and what you feel pleasant when you are there? If your answer is NO, then what can you do to make it an agreeable place? A disorganized place is the reflection of a disorderly mind. Your environment is key to being creative and powerful, it is important that you do not skip this step.

SPIRITUALITY

I believe in God, but not as one thing, not as an old man in the sky. I believe that what people call God is something in all of us. I believe that what Jesus and Mohammed and Buddha and all the rest said was right. It's just that the translations have gone wrong.

JOHN LENNON

So many times I have asked myself, how can I talk about spirituality and separate it from religion? I have great respect for the different faiths. What's more, I admire many beautiful rituals that different religions have and their approaches to explaining the essence of life and love. It is true that our logical mind can get caught up in the details of what spirituality versus religion really means, but in this book, I prefer to leave that aside and instead of referring to its structure, I prefer to talk about its content.

To say that someone is spiritual, or that I, myself, am, is the equivalent of saying I am love, I believe in love, and I practice love. The kind of love I am referring to is not specifically the romantic love between two people (although I do not exclude it), but rather the connection that all people and living beings have on this planet. Many of the concepts that I wish to share with you can create some form of conflict or intellectual confusion, so it is important to warn you that your intellect sometimes cannot explain what can only be felt and touched with the heart.

Open your heart and let´s journey into this experience, which is the basis of everything we are doing in this world.

OUR SOUL

We come into this world with the mission of healing ourselves, and through our healing, to heal the world. In our human experience we live through circumstances that support the expansion of our soul, and therefore, that of the Universe.

Our soul reaches our body, our family, our country, and a precise culture. All the elements around us sustain our mission on Earth. Nothing is by chance. When we are born, we enter this body which also contains a mind, but as we grow, we fall into a form of numbness because we have to learn to see with our human eyes. Once our physical eyes overshadow the eyes of the soul (because of socialization), that is when our healing mission begins and we recall (even in our physical experience) the reason why we came into this world at this time.

It may sound overwhelming to think that we have a great mission to accomplish. For now, we do not know how to contain ourselves and deal with difficult situations, on a day to day basis. But I do have good news for you. Your mission begins with something very simple: to live in grace, in joy and in LOVE. I am sure that, just like me, you also want this for your life.

The freedom to choose how we want to live our life is our gift, however sometimes we forget how to use this gift, at best. As I mentioned in previous chapters, we fill ourselves with fear, therefore we make choices out of fear instead of making choices with our soul. And that is when we suffer.

Why do we suffer? According to Buddha, we suffer because of our attachment to our desires. This may sound confusing because we also say that fulfilling our dreams is what expands the Universe and if we do not have objectives, then we are not evolving.

Let´s go step by step.

It is necessary to have a vision, to wish to fulfill it and to evolve with it. With each action we take, we are leading the way toward this objective. As Antonio Machado suggested, *"Travelers, there is no path, paths are made by walking."* If we do not have desires, there will be no vision, and without a vision, there will be no clear steps to take; therefore, our path can take any course and it will lead us anywhere. As the old saying goes, *"He who walks in darkness does not know where he is going."* So, do you want to go just anywhere or to a place of your choosing and where you wish to go?

The purpose of this book is to help you find your very own path, the one *you* want, not mine, not the one your parents or society dictates. I trust that the previous pages provided you with that clarity. Now that you have that clear objective, you need to check your attachment to it. This is how we prepare ourselves to win the "Hero's Journey," as author, Joseph Campbell, sets forth in his studies on mythology. Once the hero has committed to the quest, he will be faced with different rivals. Those rivals will sometimes be present in his surroundings, but most of the time they live in his mind.

One of my favorite coaches, Christine Hassler, describes very well how to bring down this rival that stops us in the hero´s journey. She says, *"The secret sauce for success is high involvement with low attachment."*

The best way to overtake fear, which becomes terrified itself when we want to progress, is through high commitment, constant action towards what we want, but very low attachment to the outcome. This is the secret: it is not desire that makes us suffer more, but rather the attachment we develop by believing that its result will label us or identify us as "enough" or "not enough." The mere thought that our essence will be compromised if we do not achieve something, is what causes our pain. In fact, our soul also suffers because from within it says, "No, we are not that achievement, we are already perfect and open, and this is only an assignment for our evolution." But we do not listen to our soul because the voice of fear is so loud and so strong when it is upset or frightened that the truth that sets us free passes before us unnoticed. The truth is that you are infinite, perfect and whole. We are not missing out on anything, we are simply frustrated by the illusions of fear. When the illusion of fear fades away, only our essence shall remain and this essence is beautiful, expansive, and abundant.

HOW TO NOT HAVE ANY ATTACHMENTS

Fear believes that we are the sum of our accomplishments (a home, a car, a trip), our diplomas (Master's, PhD, training certifications), our marital status (married, single, divorced), our economic status (amount of money in a bank account), our employment status (boss, manager, leader), the beliefs of those people who accept me (the good person, the savior of others, the courageous), and of those who "belong" in my life (my husband, my family, my children). When my identity is directly correlated with what I just mentioned, I then suffer because I am only that, the achieved desire, and if that wish is not granted or fulfilled, I simply cease being what I am.

Look how simple it is to move from a "want" to a "being."

Example: I want to own a home this year.

Reality: You were unable to buy it this year.

Conclusion: "I am not enough," "I am ashamed," "I am a failure"

So, how do I get rid of this fear that I identify with success or failure to achieve my dreams?

The answer is simple:

S U R R E N D E R.

L E T G O.

SURRENDER

If you knew who walks beside you on the way that you have chosen, fear would be impossible.
A COURSE IN MIRACLES

This surrender or letting go is not synonymous with giving up our dreams, but rather TRUSTING in something superior to us, as this beautiful phrase from *A Course in Miracles* suggests.

While it is true that our souls hold a little bit of God, a beautiful and perfect idea of the Universe, as we enter our bodies and minds to live this human experience, we become limited. This limitation helps us to fulfill our purpose, which is to live this human experience remembering every day that we are also spiritual beings. What happens is that we forget why we distract ourselves with our day-to-day struggles. That is where the real work is. And, when I refer to work, I mean "to remember" that we are part of something greater than what our human eyes and senses can perceive. We are infinite and we can access these boundless resources offered by the Universe. However, we cannot enter this vast diversity of choices and synchronicities if we are too busy relying on our own strength and our own limited human capacities.

A Course in Miracles suggests in lesson 48 "*The presence of fear is a sure sign that you are trusting in your own strength,*" and so it is; anxiety, stress, and sometimes lack of self-control arise because you forget that you are not alone, you forget to reconnect with home, to the source of your creation, to God, and only from there we will receive guidance, answers and the strength we look for in all the wrong places.

That is why we develop addictions. We attain temporary happiness through others, through drama, through food, through gambling, through working, through drugs, through alcohol, through cigarettes, through anger, and control. Without knowing that permanent happiness can only be found if we resort to our divinity.

Has it ever happened to you that you are stressed, it is Friday night, and you decide to go and relax with a few drinks? You drink more than your body needs and on Saturday morning you are not only tense because of the workload you left behind, but now your body is exhausted and emotional as a result of the short-lived pleasure you had the night before. Or perhaps, you know that you should not be with *that person* who hurts you, but inside of you, you have developed such a dependence to the momentary happiness that said person gives you, that you assent to breaking your promises and the following day you feel more empty, more depressed, and more anxious than before.

These examples can be interchanged with food, procrastination, drama, gossip, and other addictions that human beings develop seeking to fill a void with pleasurable and fleeting moments. That is why it is necessary to let go and surrender to something superior, to be able to act with a higher consciousness. Ultimately, if we continue repeating the same behavioral pattern, we will obtain exactly the same results we have always received.

HOW TO SURRENDER

Enough theory, let's get into action.

One of my favorite practices - and probably that is why I am a coach - is to translate philosophical concepts into practices and rituals that transform us into the teachers of our own lives. As Aristotle puts it: "*We are what we repeatedly do. Excellence, then, is not an act, but a habit.*" And a habit is something you do naturally after much repetition.

CREATING THE HABIT OF SURRENDERING

I recommend that you follow these steps:

1. Take responsibility for your truth. If you still do not know what your truth is and what you really want, I recommend that you return to the first chapters of this book, and diligently do the exercises. You are 100% responsible for what happens to you and nothing and no one can take away your freedom.

2. Ask for guidance. Recently I learned a delightful practice to ask for guidance. With your eyes closed, taking a few seconds to connect with your breathing, inhaling and exhaling deeply and slowly, find that unguarded space in your chest and ask your God, the Universe, the Angels or whatever you believe in, or want to invoke at that very moment: What in my life must I change to achieve what my soul desires, to fulfill my purpose on Earth? Be available to listen, it may be that your mind wants to give you many answers but be patient and recognize that divine voice that wants to speak to you. You may want to stop this exercise here or go further and deeper. When I did this exercise, I took deep breaths and I simply wrote freely. This came to me:

Love yourself. Be kind to yourself. There is no competition, only the one that your mind creates.

Trust. I am here, turn to me when you are lost in your world of ideas and thoughts. Just say: Help, I'm losing myself in my own psyche, lead me back to thoughts of love.

Open yourself. Open your heart and your presence to the world. Do not hide anything, the world needs your presence.

Everything comes when you enjoy the journey, not when you compete against yourself or against others.

Flow.

It is here that my fear dared to ask: *"And if I do flow, will there be no discipline and everything will be a disaster?"* And the answer was: *Be disciplined in all of the above and the rest will align itself.*

"Be disciplined in all of the above and the rest will align itself."

You will notice that, ironically, if you commit 100% to your inner success, external success will follow you and you will receive gifts that your mind never even planned for, or much less manipulated, on its path to them.

Next, ask for more clarity with this question: What would my life be like if I accepted and practiced all these things that you are teaching me?

In my case, I saw myself more content, more creative, more open, without attachments, more successful, softer, more feminine, and in service of others.

I no longer needed to prove myself to others but rather my validation came from within, it stemmed from the idea that if I am in this world it is because the Universe already favored me to be here, alive.

I have the green light and permission to be happy, regardless of circumstances.

3. Make your personal time non-negotiable. Personally, my mornings and my hours of sleep, over the years, have become precious, non-negotiable time frames. When I am in a constant rush, it is easy for me to disconnect and distract myself with the ideas and prejudices in my mind. That is why over time, and by learning that rituals are the secret of geniuses, I have decided to commit to two things the best way I can:

1. Time for myself in the morning.
2. Respect my hours of sleep.

I will tell you all about this personal time that I dedicate to myself in the mornings. Every morning, depending on how long I have, I try to connect with my breathing, honoring every breath of air I take as a symbol of gratitude for still being able to breathe. Once I do two to three minutes of intonation with my breathing, I take two to three minutes to give thanks. I say thank you for the smallest details and grandest things. I am grateful for the beautiful and comfortable sheets I have on my bed to realizing that there are trillions of cells inside me doing their job to make me feel good.

Once I am done being grateful for two to three minutes, I then pray. This prayer has no special pleas but rather it focuses on thankfulness again. This time I will be thankful for what I wish for, as if it already existed, because it does already exist. Everything we desire in our hearts has already been created on an invisible level. It is gratitude and visualization that allows our desires to materialize on a physical level. So, for example, as I write this book, I wake up every morning and I am grateful for its publication and for all of you who are reading it. I visualize you with this book in your hands, with a smile in your heart, feeling hopeful and motivated to move on! This is the best prayer I know! When we pray with petitions, we are suggesting and accepting that there are still non-existent, that they have not materialized ... and that simply is not true. The Universe has already created everything you asked for, now is the time for you to manifest it . I manifested you reading my book, right? This works!

Finally, as a last step, I set out my three intentions for the day, they can be as specific as: "Today I will finish writing this essay". "Today I will listen to my body before eating" or as comprehensive as: "Today I will be open to what life brings me". "Today I will give love and I will look forward to having pleasant and gentle thoughts," or you can combine the two, and by this time you will have been connected to yourself and it will be clear what intentions your soul and heart wish you to fulfill throughout your day.

4. Breathe whenever you feel you need to. So many things can go beyond our control, in fact, I would go so far as to say that everything is out of our control, and our fear does not like that at all. Let´s remember, once more, that the most important thing for fear is that we survive, and sometimes life circumstances depend on many external factors which can represent, in an unconscious and conscious manner, that our value and existence are compromised.

Since your life in that moment of anguish or fear is probably not actually in danger, but rather your mind is worrying too much about what will happen or happened (which is 99.9% of the time), then, it is time to breathe. Breathing serves several purposes. First, it puts you in control of the only thing you can be in charge of: yourself. Then, it calms your nervous system and oxygenates your brain.

When we feel disoriented by so much fear, anger, sadness, anguish, whatever your uncomfortable emotion may be, that amygdala I mentioned at the beginning of this book is activated, and although it wants you to feel you are in control, this often implies worrying too much, and it affects our immune system by the uncontrolled release of cortisol. Furthermore, it also affects the nervous system by shifting us towards negative emotional conditions, such as depression, anxiety attacks, insomnia, and chronic stress.

Let´s help our mind to feel some form of control that is much less stressful for the body with a deep inhale and a relaxing exhale. Do it as you read this, inhale deeply in a controlled fashion, hold all the oxygen for a few seconds (I call it medicine for the soul) and now release it gently. You can do this as many times as you need.

If you are able to close your eyes, you will feel much better. Some time ago I heard someone say, *"When we close our eyes, we can see more clearly because we are seeing with the eyes of the soul."*

This exercise will give you a sense of relief. Your brain will oxygenate itself and in turn, help you to think better about how to resolve that situation that overwhelms you. Moreover, your soul will receive a signal that you are finally ready to listen to it.

You are sending a message that says: "*I am lost in the thoughts of my mind. I welcome divine strength and wisdom to come into my life.*"

5. Thank you, thank you, thank you.

Energy flows where attention goes.
UNKNOWN

Do you know what one of the things that makes us feel victimized and unhappy are? The thought of scarcity: "I am not...," "I do not have...," "There is no...." or "The day I have I will.....," "When the day comes, then I will...," "When they change, then I...." The having to wait or the statement that you do not have or maybe will never have, of course makes us feel very bad. Essentially, we want to have a life abundant in love, health, money, fun, etc., and when we see that these desires cannot be fulfilled, then we feel resentful.

Even so, the important thing here is not to worry about what has not arrived yet or what you do not have. We must instead focus all of our attention to what we do have. Depending on where you place your attention, that is where your energy will be. If you focus on what you do not have or what you haven´t become yet, then your energy will be limited and scarce, creating even more of that which you do not want. When, instead, our energy is in everything we already have, we are, and we can do, we see that we are living many miracles today. That is why in step #3 "Make your personal time non-negotiable," I suggest that in your morning ritual, you practice gratitude. If you start your morning like this, then you set the tone for the entire day. However, this is not an exercise to be done only in the mornings, you can also resort to it as a rescue tool when you need it during the day.

For example: you see yourself in the mirror and you see that you still do not have that body you want. It is very easy for fear to take control and judge you. Has this happened to you? What if, instead, with your newly discovered super-awareness you say STOP – TIME FOR GRATITUDE MODE and mentally or aloud (as you prefer) begin to list everything that is great with your body: I am grateful to be healthy, today I feel no pain at all, or I am grateful to have two legs, two arms, and pretty eyes. When you begin to realize all the things that are already good, the extent of your judgment decreases and you begin to vibrate toward the direction of abundance.

Scarcity mentality makes us take for granted the many blessings that are already in our life. Remember that what is normal for you, might be considered a privilege and a luxury to someone else.

6. Have fun to flow. Happiness is the food of the soul. An existence with joyful moments and fun is a fluid and energetically magnetic existence. It may sound somewhat of an irony but it is in moments of relaxation, contentment, and fun where my best ideas have surfaced, and the same has happened to my clients who have applied it.

This happened to a client of mine named Oscar, for example. A successful businessman, he had attained professional success but lately he was in a rut, something was missing in his life, and he did not know what it was. All he knew was to work hard and unremittingly. He began his days at 7am and ended them at 7pm.

We did a lot of internal, self-discovery work and during this inner journey, we did the exercise that I taught you about beliefs. We discovered that one of his beliefs was that if he were to have fun or relax, it would suggest being irresponsible, lazy, and that his company could go bankrupt. This would imply having to let all of his employees go (which, because of his nature of wanting to help others, was a mortifying thought) and the worst-case scenario was that he was going to be left with nothing, lonely, and on the brink of death. That is why he had to work 12 hours a day, so that his worst fear would never happen.

Gradually, we began to weaken that belief by replacing it with a new belief: "*In amusement and relaxation I find high productivity and creativity.*" At first, he did not believe it, so I told him to fake it until he assimilated the new belief. To achieve this, he had to see results in order to collect new evidence that indeed it is true. That is how he decided to, little by little, take some hours off to be with himself, to breathe, to play with his daughter that he loves so much, and to simply be.

After a couple of weeks of doing so, one day in a coaching session, he excitedly told me, "*My best ideas are emerging during my fun times. The other day, I was relaxing in my jacuzzi at home and suddenly, a business idea arose that is not only good, but I have everything to start it up without any stress. I will take it on as a hobby and the best thing is that I will provide jobs to people in the surrounding area. I am beginning to feel that enthusiasm that I thought I had lost by spending hours in my business doing the same thing every day, aimlessly. I was in survival mode.*"

AHA!

In those moments of nurturing the soul is when it tells you what to do, from there on you connect with your inspiration, and motivation and enthusiasm are born. True equilibrium or balance stems from being able to have fun and work at the same time. There will come a day where there is no difference between one and the other. Perhaps in a season you will work very hard to carry out a project, but if that project originates from your inspiration, then it will not matter because you will be having fun and creating at the same time.

Likewise, when you sense beforehand (with your newly awakened awareness) that you must relax and enjoy yourself, by walking, sharing time with family, meditating, etc., surely you will. When our soul is happy, we are highly productive. This is the best thing you can do to for your finances, your business, your career, and your personal relationships. Have a good time in an outstanding business. Allow yourself to rest and have fun and you will see the magical ideas and answers that will arise from these pauses. You will create the most important thing: a passionate life where work and amusement will become one.

In his last coaching session, Oscar told me: *"I am still busy, but I work on new projects that come about when I go to my farm on the weekends. It is there that a new project connects with me, and yes, it is work, but what I do gives me so much pleasure, that I feel free and happy."*

7. Eat well and exercise. Our body is our vehicle, a beautiful and intelligent temple that we were given in which take this journey of the human experience. That is why, for some time now, I stopped viewing the body as something with which I had to compete or mistreat in order to be thinner, to push to endure more hours awake or to subject it to many hours of inactivity sitting in front of a computer.

Few human beings learn to have a healthy relationship with their body. From the moment we are born, the media bombards us with notions about how we should look and what we need to do to achieve this ideal even if it is detrimental to our health. No need to look further than the typical picture of a couple, with perfect bodies, expensive clothes, luxurious accessories expressing power and joy. I have nothing against material possessions that give us pleasure or against caring for our body to be vibrant and healthy. The problem with this image is that it depicts a perfection that immediately causes us to compare ourselves to it and say, "They are happy because they have it all, money, beauty, and things. On the other hand, I am inadequate because I do not look like that, nor do I have all of those items. I must then postpone my happiness, I must work long hours although this goes against my health."

Enough!

Taking care of our body should not have a superficial connotation, this should be directly linked with spirituality. Taking care of yourself is a spiritual practice because it is the way we say to the Universe:

"Thank you for giving me this body that allows me to go from one place to another, to represent myself to create,

to serve, to grow. I am so grateful for it that I demonstrate this appreciation to you by caring for it and honoring it."

There is also another syndrome caused by these images that we perceive, which seeks to take care of the body in an obsessive and compulsive manner, because we must fill a void or we have some form of distortion with our body image. I know a lot about this disorder because I actually experienced it. I know that you can go to extremes to the point of refraining yourself from eating and overexerting your body with exercise by causing it the same damage as one who does nothing.

"So, Paola, what do I do? Do I take care of myself or not?"

It is all part of our intention. That is why this suggestion pertains to the chapter on how to be spiritually active. If we perceive that eating healthy and exercising has the same intention as a spiritual act, then we discover another way to connect with our source, another form of loving ourselves and enjoying this perfect vehicle that was given to us. When we commit to eating healthy and exercising, we essentially give ourselves joy. It is then that this practice becomes a gratifying and spiritual experience. It is important to keep in mind that this is not bound to simply going to the gym and becoming a vegetarian, or following a Paleo diet, or any other diet fad. You must discover what you enjoy doing, find out your favorite way to move. Likewise with food, you must use self examination and see what types of foods fill you with energy and vitality.

For a long time, I did not eat any animal products and felt good about it as a matter of principle; however, recently, I started to include chicken and eggs into my diet and I feel incredible. These are different stages of my life and I wish to continue swaying between them, but with love and inner peace, and without any form of dogmatism that makes me feel constrained or out of control.

As I mentioned before, to get to know oneself is a privilege and a pleasure. That is why I invite you to find out how you enjoy exercising and how your body feels eating certain foods, so you may finally commit to this lifestyle. You will soon discover that with a well-nourished and exercised body, your soul will be comfortable living within it. Our body is the home that contains our being, it is well worth cleansing it, caring for it, fixing it, and embellishing it. You will live happily, peacefully, and assured that you are in a safe and healthy place.

Furthermore, you will be vibrating so highly that everything you wish for will stick to you as if you were a miracle magnet. Money, relationships, business deals, ideas, love, peace, plenitude and everything will be at your disposal because you will be energized to receive and create without limitations.

8. Find your tribe. Your tribe are the people with whom you surround yourself, preferably people who are vibrating like you or similarly. People who appreciate the same thing you do and that you can turn to when you are faltering.

Without my tribe, consisting of people who know my vision of life and my philosophy, I could not even do half of what I achieve. They listen to me when I need them, they guide me when I am lost in my own fear, and they hold me accountable when I set my mind on something.

You share a spiritual contract with your tribe. They are in your life not by chance, we attract these people because there is purpose. As suggested in the book, *A Course in Miracles*, "All encounters are holy" and "Interpersonal relationships are sacred assignments."

We should not be in this alone. Nurturing and sharing with your tribe is also a spiritual practice that connects you with your being by bonding with others. In the end, all human beings are here to connect with others; this gives us a sense of belonging and makes us happier.

At a spiritual level, we are all part of the same source that was separated into different forms of energy and personified in this body that we now have; however, if we give it some thought, we are all one, we are brothers and sisters who, when we share and help each other, we potentiate consciousness and connection with our source.

Never isolate yourself, find your tribe and care for it as you would a beautiful and delicate plant. The benefits are incredibly healing and spiritual.

9. Connect yourself with nature. Ten years ago, I came across a sport that changed my life: surfing. When I discovered it, I lived in the city and passionate about it as I was, I would go surfing every weekend at the beach closest to San José, my city at the time. After a few months, it no longer was just a hobby, it became essential for me to practice, and when I stayed in the city, I felt incomplete without understanding why.

Years later, I had the chance to live close to the beach in Brazil. The most incredible thing was that, despite my love of surfing, I was not surfing every day. I did, however, enjoy walking on the beach, proving to myself the incredible power that nature had on my emotions. Whenever I felt bad, I would go outside, I would look at the ocean or go surfing and it seemed that my problems dissipated, or at the very least, they did not have the same dimension as my fear had portrayed them to have.

My wise father always said the same, but I never really understood it when I was growing up. I saw how his weekends were devoted to his farm. During the week, he worked downtown at his business in the city, and when the weekend arrived, he could not think of anything more enjoyable than to be in his farm, to sow, to plow, to simply do anything in those surroundings. He would invite us to go with him, but seeing that we were not on the same level of consciousness, he respected our wishes and went to the farm alone. He would say: *"It is to my utmost gratification that the weekend comes around and I can work the land in my farm."* It was years later that I discovered the incredible power that nature has on our energy vibration and the connection with this creative source, with God.

That is why I invite you to connect with nature. You do not have to go to the beach like I do. If you do not like the beach or for some geographical or financial reason you cannot go to one, just go out on your lunch break (if you work in an office) and look for a tree, sit under it, observe the greenery around you, look at the leaves that hang from it, and fill yourself with its vibration. God is there!

On weekends, try to discover new places, go to the ocean, go to the mountains, anywhere, really, where is not too much cement and you will notice how you return to work on Monday recharged and happy.

I think sometimes we believe that spirituality is merely praying, going to church or meditating, but it is much more than that. When we learn to contemplate all the abundance that Universe gives us through nature, this also becomes a beautiful and pleasant spiritual practice. Love and beauty is in all places and in all elements of nature, let´s connect with this Force to set us free.

10. Practice mindfulness.

If you are not in the here and in the now, then how are you going to reach that future that you long for?
ALBERTO ROMANO

These were wise words that I got from my coach (that's right, as a coach, I have my own coach, too) when he notices that I am in an anxiety frenzy because I live too much in my future. This advice, even if it is my last suggestion, is certainly not the least important of them all. In fact, I can tell you that this last practice is the basis for all others. Generally, we live in the past or in the future, setting off a great deal of sadness or resentment because we cannot change what has already happened or because, like me, we are too preoccupied with controlling our future.

In my case, by multitasking and being too passionate, my mind can enter into a sea of projects and business ideas, which most of the time, even though I am very enthusiastic, can also make me feel very overwhelmed. I get overwhelmed wanting to do a lot, change, improve, have more, and be more. And that is why I have a hard time connecting and focusing on one thing, since so many projects distract and divert me.

Ironically, learning to be in the here and in the now, focused on a single task, is what allows me to move forward faster, as the famous catchphrase in Spanish says, *"Slowly please, I am in a hurry."* For example, writing this book and finishing it was an act of complete centering in the present, without judgments, without agenda, simply sitting down to guide the information I have received through my experiences, my profession, and my connection with my Creative Source. Whenever I got distracted, the project was postponed, but as soon as I remembered my mission with acceptance and patience, I wrote one word at a time. This is what brings me back to my Source when I become unfocused thanks to the thousands of ideas and biases that explode in my head day by day.

How to do it?

Well, with this book you realized what your vision of the future is, who you are, and where you are going. I trust that you are already clear of what your heart longs for and what small steps you must take to get there.

So, it is time now for conscious and unhurried action.

Take every task of your life, and as best you can, focus on what you are doing, turn off distractions, and connect with the present.

I talked about breathing before; be in complete awareness of your breathing for a few seconds, feel as the air comes in and out of you, contemplate how each part of your body feels, connect with the sounds around you, and stay there silently.

You are in the here and in the now.

What is currently happening is the only thing we have at this time and this moment is as unique as the one that follows, and the one after, and the one after that. Let´s learn to contemplate nature, to be mindful of our breathing and of other people; everything has something to teach us, yet nothing will permeate a mind that is surrounded by noise.

What should you do today? Set your mind that will put all your focus on at least one task of the day, do it with the intention of connecting with the moment, with the task, with your presence, with your intelligence, and with your intuition. When we live in the present, we can also detach ourselves from the results. If we are too identified with our expectations, then we do not experience what we are living in the now and we spend our lives without actually enjoying it.

Why do we enjoy being in love so much? Because when we are in those first stages of discovery of one another, you are present, all your senses are connected in the moment, absorbing every single moment with that person. It is gratifying, unreserved and pleasant, that is why we enjoy it so much. Imagine living your life as if you were in love with each moment, absorbing, observing, and taking advantage of what is in front of us.

This is a lifestyle. I would love to tell you that once you learn this you will apply it every day and remember it forever. But then again, sometimes you will overlook it and when you are disconnected or going through a crisis, you will dredge it up again. The important thing here is not perfection, but to always aspire for a spiritual connection.

ENJOY THE JOURNEY

With the love that emerges from my heart, I have just shared with you what has set me FREE and I know that in your journey you will find this same experience.

For me, freedom is not the destination but the journey itself. Enough with postponing your happiness and your freedom, life would be too dreary and boring if everything occurred just like our fear presumes it will. The Universe has wonderful and awesome ways of working, everything happens in a perfect way, in perfect time. Everything is part of the synchronicity in which we live in and to flow in this synchronicity is the true secret.

As long as we flow with everything that happens for us, trusting that every single thing has a purpose, then the Universe shall provide us with the answers, with ease, and with clarity.

My intention in this book has been to offer you all the tools I know, teach you to apply them, to combine them with what you, yourself, already know, and with other teachings that you will acquire along the way, in order to create your own formula for freedom.

Remember that all the answers are at your disposal and the more you practice silence, the more you curiously contemplate what transpires, and the more you connect with your soul, the more you shall secure a life of plenitude. Perhaps never perfect, but intensely beautiful and unique in all of its imperfections. Also, keep in mind that you are not alone in this, there are already millions of people in the world in this same quest; start by vibrating high and you will attract them to you. And if you feel alone for some reason, remember that you are only as far as a conscious breath from home, from yourself, and you know that when you are with yourself, you are never alone. When you are with yourself you are FREE.

NOTES

NOTES

NOTES

NOTES

NOTES

NOTES

NOTES

NOTES

Made in the USA
Middletown, DE
02 August 2019